NEW TESTAMENT MESSAGE

A Biblical-Theological Commentary

Wilfrid Harrington, O.P. and Donald Senior, C.P.

EDITORS

New Testament Message, Volume 14

PHILIPPIANS AND PHILEMON

Mary Ann Getty, R.S.M.

Michael Glazier, Inc.
Wilmington, Delaware

MICHAEL GLAZIER, INC.
1210A King Street
Wilmington, Delaware 19806

Library of Congress Catalog Card Number: 80-65637
International Standard Book Number
    New Testament Message series: 0-89453-123-9
    PHILIPPIANS AND PHILEMON: 0-89453-137-9

Printed in the United States of America by Abbey Press

Contents

DEDICATION

To my students from whom I have learned so much, and especially to Connie, Holly, Gail, Maureen, Jeanie, Carole, Nanette and Theresa—all friends of Fanny.

EDITORS' PREFACE

New Testament Message is a commentary series designed to bring the best of biblical scholarship to a wide audience. Anyone who is sensitive to the mood of the church today is aware of a deep craving for the Word of God. This interest in reading and praying the scriptures is not confined to a religious elite. The desire to strengthen one's faith and to mature in prayer has brought Christians of all types and all ages to discover the beauty of the biblical message. Our age has also been heir to an avalanche of biblical scholarship. Recent archaeological finds, new manuscript evidence, and the increasing volume of specialized studies on the Bible have made possible a much more profound penetration of the biblical message. But the flood of information and its technical nature keeps much of this scholarship out of the hands of the Christian who is eager to learn but is not a specialist. *New Testament Message* is a response to this need.

The subtitle of the series is significant: "A Biblical-Theological Commentary." Each volume in the series, while drawing on up-to-date scholarship, concentrates on bringing to the fore in understandable terms the specific message of each biblical author. The essay-format (rather than a word-by-word commentary) helps the reader savor the beauty and power of the biblical message and, at the same time, understand the sensitive task of responsible biblical interpretation.

A distinctive feature of the series is the amount of space given to the "neglected" New Testament writings, such as Colossians, James, Jude, the Pastoral Letters, the Letters of Peter and John. These briefer biblical books make a significant but often overlooked contribution to the richness of the New Testament. By assigning larger than normal coverage to these books, the series hopes to give these parts of Scripture the attention they deserve.

Because *New Testament Message* is aimed at the entire English speaking world, it is a collaborative effort of international proportions. The twenty-two contributors represent biblical scholarship in North America, Britain, Ireland and Australia. Each of the contributors is a recognized expert in his or her field, has published widely, and has been chosen because of a proven ability to communicate at a popular level. And, while all of the contributors are Roman Catholic, their work is addressed to the Christian community as a whole. The New Testament is the patrimony of all Christians.It is the hope of all concerned with this series that it will bring a fuller appreciation of God's saving Word to his people.

Wilfrid Harrington, O.P.
Donald Senior, C.P.

GENERAL INTRODUCTION

The problems of the first century church were not so very different from our own. Much as we would wish to think that with our developed twentieth century mentality we have eluded them, problems of morality, divisions along the lines of social, political, liturgical, doctrinal values, crises of leadership and followship, of people enslaving other people, of persons' refusing responsibility for creating a more human world continue to plague us. Inspired words from a first century prophet, the apostle Paul, who called himself a "servant of Jesus Christ" (Phil 1:1) and a "prisoner for the Lord" (Philemon 1:1) can help us. Paul is a model for the pastoral care many today long for. He is a friend who experienced much of the same anguish we feel when we do not feel free.

Writing probably between 57-63 A.D. from Ephesus, Paul composed Philippians and Philemon, letters of extraordinary relevance for our times. The letters addressed to the Philippians and to Philemon count among the so-called "captivity" epistles, correspondence Paul is reputed to have sent from imprisonment. For many reasons, Colossians, Ephesians and Philemon have been compared with one another more often than Philippians and Philemon. The authors of Colossians and Philemon, Paul and Timothy, as well as the greetings of Paul's companions at the end of these letters, have been identified as the same. Colossians has been compared to Ephesians almost as an outline to the more refined finished draft.

Nevertheless, short and personal as it is, Philemon has a similarity of vocabulary with Colossians and many interpreters identify their deliverer as the same person. But as much of a case can be made for considering Philippians and Philemon together, with Colossians and Ephesians forming a separate problem. Philippians and Philemon both seem to have been written from prison by Paul or by a close companion writing under Paul's name. They are both documents of contemporary value because they appeal to the kind of corporate witness that is so needed in today's highly compartmentalized world. They are both challenging documents because they urge our communities as well as those to whom they were originally addressed to face the issues that divide us, to act with an upright moral conscience, to resist divisiveness and to listen more attentively to the Spirit that calls us to unity and to greater generosity.

Hardly anyone doubts that Colossians and Ephesians were penned by the same hand, Ephesians being a slightly longer and probably later development of the ideas that are in Colossians. The author claims to be Paul writing from prison circumstances. The content and structure of Ephesians is parallel to Colossians and the two epistles have more than eighty common terms that are unique to these two epistles. But emphasis on the risen and exalted Christ as well as on the glorified image of the universal church distinguishes the Christology and ecclesiology of Colossians and Ephesians from that of Philippians and Philemon. Therefore, although tradition identifies Rome as the place of all four of these captivity epistles, there are serious reasons for reexamining this question, particularly regarding Philippians, the first epistle we shall consider in this commentary.

Philippians

AN INTRODUCTION
TO PHILIPPIANS

THE TRADITIONAL consensus among interpreters is that Philippians and Philemon, along with Ephesians and Colossians were written from Rome where Paul was under house arrest, as Acts testify (28:16-30). Indeed, the author of these epistles identifies himself as "Paul, a prisoner for the Lord" (Eph 4:1; cf. 3:1; Phil 1:7,13; Col 1:24; 4:10; Philemon 1:1). There are certain indications in Philippians that suggest a Roman origin: Paul refers in chapter one to the praetorian guard (1:13) and in his farewell sends greetings from "all of Caesar's household" (4:22). These references reinforced scholarly opinion that Paul writes from Rome where the praetorian guard headquartered and where Paul could have evangelized members of the emperor's own family. Nevertheless, there are certain nagging problems that point to a place of origin for Philippians closer to Philippi and to a date earlier than the other captivity epistles, perhaps considerably earlier than Ephesians and Colossians with their special vocabulary and well developed Christology.

Philippians indicates that members of the Philippian community paid several visits to Paul (Phil 4:1-10; cf. 2:19-30) so that travel back and forth must have been rather easy. Since journeys between Rome and Philippi would have required a month to six weeks, a location nearer to Philippi, Ephesus, for example, suits better the general impression that it was not so very difficult for the Philippians to send envoys bearing gifts to Paul, nor for Paul to promise to send Epaphroditus and Timothy to Philippi (2:19,25). The journey between Ephesus and Philippi is estimated to have required only about a week. Although Acts does not witness to Paul's imprisonment in Ephesus, the apostle himself testifies that he faced death in Asia (1 Cor 15:30-32; 2 Cor 1:8-10). It is evident from the letter to the Philippians that a threat of imminent death is a very serious possibility for the author.

Not only has the Roman origin and the date of Philippians been a matter of debate, but even Paul's authorship and the reality of his imprisonment at the time of this writing have been seriously questioned by interpreters. For many great people an experience of imprisonment and even the threat of death only serve to strengthen their commitment and resolve. Indeed from the early Christian martyrs to the courageous example of a Thomas More or a Martin Luther King, the dominant impression is that not only firm conviction, but even *joy* characterize the period of confinement, undoubtedly much to the consternation of their jailers. Some commentators suggest that the zealous apostle Paul could not have authored the epistle to the Philippians from prison because the tone is so serene and joy is one of the characteristic terms of the epistle. Actually, a closer reading shows how intensely Paul suffered from the uncertainty of his own future and the future of his ministry even while he tenaciously holds on to his faith and hope. The Paul of Philippians seems to be torn between confidence that he will be liberated and fear that he will not be. Not that Paul is afraid to die as he testifies in Phil 1:21: "For me to live is Christ and to die is gain." Nevertheless he betrays a real anxiety about his future, especially for the sake of the Philippians (1:24) and his unfinished work in the service of the gospel.

The consistent emphasis of Philippians is that the community there should strive for greater unity. The Philippians were inclined to be factious and divisive. Philippi enjoyed great prominence as a Roman colony and its people were proud of their Roman citizenship (cf. Acts 16:12). Philippian Christians were particularly generous in showing concern and financially aiding Paul. They had been especially blessed in their ministers: Paul, Timothy, (1:1, 2:19-24), Epaphroditus (2:25-30). The mutual affection between these apostles and the community is very clear. Nevertheless, Paul returns again and again to stress the dangers of disharmony and the necessity to strengthen the bonds of community.

Two main themes dominate the epistle to the Philippians, ideas that will be treated in this commentary where they seem to be most relevant for understanding Paul. First there is the theme of *community* (the *koinonia*) which Paul consistently challenges his addressees to make stronger. This insistence is buttressed by Paul's emphasis on universality: he loves *all* the Philippians (1:7-8; 4:21) and urges them to singleness of mind and heart (1:27; 2:5; 4:2). The second pervasive theme of Philippians is that of *joy* emphasized with the frequent imperative "Rejoice" (1:4, 18, 19,25; 2:2, 17,18,28,29; 4:1,4,10). The community of faith in the gospel of Christ is the motivation for Paul's undauntable joyfulness.

PAUL AND TIMOTHY:
SERVANTS OF CHRIST JESUS.
(1:1-2).

> **1** Paul and Timothy, servants of Christ Jesus,
> To all the saints in Christ Jesus who are at Philippi, with the bishops and deacons;
> ²Grace to you and peace from God our Father and the Lord Jesus Christ.

Paul, the pastor and apostle, addresses the Philippians with great affection, betraying already in these first verses the closeness of feeling he has for them. As he does in 1 and 2 Corinthians, Colossians and Philemon, Paul includes

Timothy who, according to Acts, would be well-known to the community at Philippi as Paul's beloved companion (cf. Acts 16:1-3,10,13; 19:22; 20:1-4). Both Paul and Timothy are designated "servants of Jesus Christ," a title that emphasizes the kind of complete, generous service to the gospel that Paul enjoins upon all Christians, and especially on the community at Philippi as Paul will reiterate throughout this epistle (see, for example 2:4-5; 3:17; 4:1-3, 14-16,21). With this designation Paul also underscores the fact that he and Timothy have together received the same calling.

In almost every other Pauline epistle (except 2 Thessalonians and 1 Timothy), Paul begins by introducing himself as an "apostle of Jesus Christ." Elsewhere when the self-designation "servant of Christ Jesus" appears (cf. Rom 1:1), it is supplemented by the title "apostle." Normally, Paul is quite adamant in his defense of his own apostolic authority because his commission to preach the gospel is based on a divine vocation. But the word "apostle" appears only once in Philippians (2:25), referring to Epaphroditus as messenger of the Philippians rather than to any call from God. The substitution of "servant" and deletion of "apostle" in Paul's introduction could signify several things. The "servant" designation is consistent with the message of the letter which implores Christians to imitate Christ in taking the "form of a slave" (Phil 2:7). Paul could also be trying to identify closely with Timothy as well as with the Philippians because of their common calling. He is implying that he and Timothy can serve as models for the Philippians in their mutual service. Furthermore, in writing to a community obviously linked to himself by bonds of mutual affection, Paul might not have needed nor wanted to stress his authority so much as his servanthood. In any case, the humility implicit in the title "servant" fits well the tone and message of this epistle.

Paul, with his comrade Timothy, addresses the members of the Philippian community as "saints," praying for their peace, speaking of joyful thanksgiving for all of them. Timothy is the son of a mixed marriage (Acts 16:1-3), his mother is a Jewess (2 Tim 1:5) and his father a Greek. Timothy was uncircumcized until he joined Paul's apostolic team. Apparently the reason Paul encouraged his circumcision was so that Timothy could more completely validate his mission in the eyes of some Jewish-Christian leaders (Acts 16:3-4). Exactly why Paul thought this necessary in the light of the fact that it occurs after the Jerusalem decree exempting Gentile converts from the necessity of circumcision (Acts 15:22-29) is not apparent. But consistency is not one of the more frequent accusations levelled against Paul. In fact, writing to the Galatians, Paul strenuously insists that neither circumcision nor uncircumcision make any difference (cf. Gal 3:28; 5:6; 6:15). But perhaps the circumcision of Timothy, if it could provide a means of making his mission more acceptable to certain significant authorities and therefore, more effective, could have seemed to the "servants of Christ Jesus," a small price to pay.

Paul evidently had more confidence in Timothy than the younger man had in himself. Gently Paul admonishes his convert not to allow his natural timidity to interfere with the forcefulness of his vocation (cf. 1 Cor 16:10-11). Timothy must have evidenced special gifts of prophetic utterance that qualified him as an authority in the church (1 Tim 1:18; 4:14) despite his youth (1 Tim 4:12). He is held in particular esteem, especially in the church of Ephesus (1 Tim 1:3). Paul appreciated Timothy's vocation and his service to the church, as is indicated not only in this epistle to the Philippians (2:19-24) but also in the fact that Timothy was entrusted with special assignments as ambassador for Paul (1 Thess 3:2; 1 Cor 4:17) and that Timothy seems to have accompanied Paul on his second and third missionary journeys (Acts 16:3; 20:4).

It appears, according to Luke's account in Acts, that Timothy first met Paul at Lystra during the missionary journey Paul undertook in obedience to the voice he heard in a dream commanding him to "Come to Macedonia and help us" (Acts 16:9). There Timothy was circumcized and then he joined Paul and Silas (probably the same as Silvanus, cf. 1 Thess 1:1; 2 Thess 1:1). They proceeded to Philippi via the important town of Troas where Luke joined them (cf. Acts 16:10-17; 20:5-21; 27:1-28). In Philippi, Lydia, a prominent citizen, was baptized along with all of her household and invited the travelers to share her hospitality as many of the women of the New Testament are depicted as doing in response to the gospel preaching (Acts 16:13-15; cf. Lk 7:36-50; 8:1-3; 10:38-42; Jn 2:1-11; 12:1-8).

According to Luke's account in Acts (16:16-40), Paul's exorcism of a young, fortune-telling slave woman prompted her owners to instigate legal action against the apostle and his companions. Unhappy with their sudden loss of revenue, the owners charged foul play and succeeded in having Paul and Silas punished with a beating. When authorities tried to add the indignity that the two should be secretively expelled from the city, Paul protested that he was a Roman citizen and that he wanted the unjust matter made public. Frightened, the magistrates went to Paul and entreated him and his companions to leave Philippi. Paul acquiesced only after a farewell visit to Lydia's household and to all the "brethren" there (Acts 16:40).

Despite the unpleasant experiences of harassment, imprisonment and expulsion, the enduring impression one receives about the community at Philippi, especially from Paul's own words in this epistle, is that it is with this community that Paul experiences his deepest relationship—this church, more than any other, continues to offer aid and affection even while Paul prompts them to greater cohesion.

Paul greets "all the saints in Christ Jesus who are at Philippi . . . ." This is an all encompassing greeting, for it becomes increasingly clear from a careful reading of this epistle, that this is a special community, docile to the Spirit, faithful and persevering in grace. Who are those Paul designates as "saints?" In Romans, the answer is more explicit: "We know that in everything God works for good with those who love him, who are called according to his purpose. For those whom he foreknew, he also predestined to be conformed to the image of his son, in order that he might be the first born among many brethren. And those whom he predestined, he also called; and those whom he called he also justified; and those whom he justified he also glorified" (Rom 8:28-30).

In Philippians, in addition to the "saints," those who serve them as special functionaries are addressed: the administrators, the bishops and deacons. This allusion to offices which are sometimes considered to be more characteristic of a post-Pauline ecclesiastical institution has suggested to some interpreters that Philippians postdates the apostle Paul or that these terms were a later addition. Nevertheless, in Romans, the *chef-d'oeuvre* of Paul's writings, the deacon Phoebe is mentioned (cf. Rom 16:1-2). Furthermore, although many consider the Pastoral epistles to be of dubious Pauline authorship, the rather well-developed description of these and other roles within the church administration in these comparatively early writings implies that they were implemented fairly quickly as needs within the primitive Christian community developed (cf. 1 Tim 3:1-10; Titus 1:6-16). Luke's reference in Acts 6:1-6 supports the idea of an early decision to ordain deacons to administer the community's goods for the sake of the poor. It also seems reasonable to assume that if one of the purposes for Paul's writing this letter was to thank his Philippian benefactors (see Phil 4:10-18), Paul would include a reference to the administrators of the community. In any case, it is not necessary to assign too rigid a connotation to these offices at the time of the writing of Philippians.

"Grace and peace" are the messianic blessings bestowed on the saints. These are gifts from God who begot Jesus, who is Lord. Combining the Jewish blessing of "peace" to the Greek and Latin preference for joy (i.e., prosperity), Paul christens his greeting in his own characteristic style (cf. Rom 1:7; 1 Cor 1:3; 2 Cor 1:2; Gal 1:3; Eph 1:2; 1 Thess 1:1; 2 Thess 1:2; Titus 1:4). These are the blessings "poured forth into our hearts by the Holy Spirit" (Rom 5:5). These are bestowed on us from Jesus who, having reconciled us, making us at peace with God (Rom 5:1), draws us near to God so that we dare to call him *Abba*, Father (Rom 8:15)!

PARTNERSHIP IN THE GOSPEL.
(1:3-11).

[3]I thank my God in all my remembrance of you, [4]always in every prayer of mine for you all making my prayer with joy, [5]thankful for your partnership in the gospel from the first day until now. [6]And I am sure that he who began a good work in you will bring it to completion at the day of Jesus Christ. [7]It is right for me to feel thus about you all, because I hold you in my heart, for you are all partakers with me of grace, both in my imprisonment and in the defence and confirmation of the gospel. [8]For God is my witness, how I yearn for you all with the affection of Christ Jesus. [9]And it is my prayer that your love may abound more and more, with knowledge and all discernment, [10]so that you may approve what is excellent, and may be pure and blameless for the day of Christ, [11]filled with the fruits of righteousness which come through Jesus Christ, to the glory and praise of God.

These verses are rich in the beautiful thoughts typical of Philippians. Thanksgiving, joy, solidarity of community in the gospel: these are ideas that reverberate throughout the epistle. Paul's friends in Philippi give him cause for thanks. They have been generous and faithful to the gospel. They have been prodigal in showing their devotion for Paul by sending him gifts (cf. 4:10) and relaying messages about their concern. Paul is particularly grateful for the

Philippians "partnership in the gospel." More important than their generosity in sharing material things is their fidelity to the good news. While they demonstrate with gifts and messages their love for Paul from time to time, their sharing responsibility for the gospel is in the *constancy* of their lives. The faithfulness of their lives explains how Paul's *prayer* of thanksgiving can be constant.

Community

The Philippians' "partnership" with Paul in the gospel underscores another familiar Pauline notion. Far from being the "superlative" apostle (cf. 2 Cor 11:5) who is removed from his communities, Paul frequently refers to his "team ministry." His is an apostolate shared with others. He introduced his comrade Timothy in the first line of the epistle as if eager to include him in the affection and success he himself experienced with the Philippians. But Paul does not restrict his sharing to a few. Aware that he has no monopoly on ministry and that his own needs for support and friendship are significant, Paul expresses his gratitude for the *koinonia*, for "community" in the gospel.

Community in the abstract sense of a simple bonding of Christians together in friendship is never found in Paul's writings. For him, community is created when believers participate in the gospel, embracing the good news with eagerness to communicate it to others. Rather than being a subjective experience of mutual friendliness, the community of Christians for Paul is composed of those responsive to and responsible for the gospel mission.

The concept of community is a very strong, very important one for Paul. The bond of fellowship outweighs every other consideration. Differences threatened the early Christian communities just as they continue to plague the church today. There were arguments about dietary laws (1 Cor 8:1-13; 10:23-30), and the keeping of feasts. There were liturgical abuses (1 Cor 11:17-34), blatant immorality (1 Cor 5:1-13), Christians even taking their disputes to civil courts (1 Cor 6:1-11). The "weak" and the "strong" were mutually judgmental (1 Cor 8:7-9; Rom 14:1-23). There were crises of discipleship and, probably much more scandalous, the crises of leadership (see the confrontation between Peter and Paul described by Paul in Galatians 2:11-14). Despite the pain involved, despite the conviction that some were, in fact, objectively in the right, despite the need for confrontation, Paul insists that the communion resulting from unity of faith is to remain the overriding factor in reconciling all members.

Community is the glue that reconciles members of local churches and also calls each member to greater generosity. Needs (cf. 1 Cor 11:17-34) as well as gifts (1 Cor 12:1-31; 14:1-40; Rom 12:1-21) threaten to divide the church. But charity is the love of the very Spirit of God "poured out in our hearts" (Rom 5:5) enabling us not only to be reconciled but to be ambassadors of reconciliation (2 Cor 5:20). Without the Spirit of charity, differences would separate us, but charity enables community whereby sharing of faith overcomes differences.

That is what Paul elsewhere calls the great *mystery* of God's working in the world (cf. Rom 11:25). The circle widens as Paul returns again and again to this idea of the centrality of community. Jews can no longer exclude the Gentiles and Gentiles cannot lord it over the Jews. "In Christ there is neither Jew nor Greek, there is neither slave nor free, there is neither male nor female, for you are all one in Christ Jesus" (Gal 3:28). Now in Christ, "you who once were far off have been brought near in the blood of Christ. For he is our peace, who has made us both one and has broken down the dividing wall of hostility" (Eph 2:13-14). This is the mystery of the reconciliation of all in Christ that prompts Paul to cry out in praise of God, "O the depth of the riches and wisdom and knowledge of God" (Rom 11:33), and elsewhere to ask rhetorically, "What can separate us" (Rom 8:35)? The community of faith is greater than any differences.

Such a concept of community permeates Philippians. Despite their affection for Paul, despite their generous aid, their concern for Epaphroditus, and their fidelity to Paul's teachings, divisiveness threatens them and painful disputes haunt them (e.g. 4:2-3). But Paul recalls them to the fundamental "teaching" of the gospel—accepting the God and Father of Jesus Christ means accepting one another as brothers and sisters.

The Philippians have held firmly to the faith "from the first day" which means from the time of their initial conversion. Better understanding of this phrase comes when it is related to what Paul says in 4:15: "And you Philippians know that *in the beginning of the gospel* . . . you entered into partnership with me . . . ." In a sense, the gospel actually begins with the public ministry of Jesus (Mark 1:1). But for Paul, the gospel is "the power of salvation" (Rom 1:16), so that its "first day" is the moment a community experiences its salvation power. Paul refers to the Philippians' openness in receiving the word and to their fidelity in keeping it. In this way they become collaborators. Their faithfulness continues "until now," signifying that the Philippians presently continue to preach the gospel through their lives.

Paul calls on God to be his martyr, his witness to the greatness of his love (Rom 1:19; 2 Cor 1:23; 1 Thess 2:5,10). The apostle expresses the depth of his love for the Philippians, saying he loves them with the affection of Jesus Himself. This intimate love shows no partiality but embraces *all* those in the community. Thus Paul continues to emphasize the note of universality that will become so central in chapter two. The community embraces *all* the members; none can be excluded from the mutual bonds that unite it to the ministry of the gospel.

The work God *began* in the Philippians will be finished "on the day of Christ." All leads toward this day, the time of the *parousia*, the second coming of Christ. It is God who began and God who finishes the work of the gospel; it is not the result of human endeavor. This idea is echoed in 2:13

when Paul says, "God is at work in you." What God is working through the Philippians is "good" (cf. 1:6).

The content of Paul's prayer (v.9) makes it a model for Christians' expressed and unexpressed yearning. The mutual *agape* (love) Christians share will spill over into greater understanding and perception so that they will be able to embrace whatever is good to the point of excellence, whatever is pure, whatever is blameless (see 4:4-9). Knowledge or understanding for Paul is not mere intellectual assent but the commitment of an obedient heart. Knowledge is fidelity. And Christians grow in the knowledge of God exhibited in greater understanding of the responsibilities of community.

When the *RSV* translates Paul's ardent hope that the Philippians may "*approve*" what is excellent, pure and blameless, it aptly conveys the meaning of the verb that means "to test and then accept as tested." Thus he speaks, for example, in Rom 12:2, of "approving the will of God." The "more excellent" way of 1 Cor 13 prompted the hymn of charity, a gift that exceeds all others. The pure and blameless appear almost as synonyms although, in Greek, the term for "pure" connotes sincerity which could continue the idea of testing for approval, while the term "blameless" is closer to "obedience."

Righteousness, a term synonymous with justification, is a central Pauline theme, developed most extensively in the epistle to the Romans. Righteousness comes through faith in Christ (cf. 3:9), it is not the result of works or human merit. Here in Philippians Paul puts the same idea a little differently, speaking of the "fruits of righteousness which come through Jesus Christ." Righteousness is gift/grace. The fruits of righteousness, characterizing a life lived for God, are so many expressions of the fruits of the Spirit: love, joy, peace, patience, kindness, goodness, faithfulness, gentleness, self-control (Gal 5:22). The beginning of salvation is the justification that comes from faith. Salvation itself is the grace-filled life that bears the fruit of righteousness.

IN ALL THINGS CHRIST IS PROCLAIMED.
(1:12-30).

Philippians 1:12-30 encompasses three subsections centering around the dominant thought expressed in verse 18: "In every way . . . Christ is proclaimed and in that I rejoice." each of the subsections refers to a very painful dilemma Paul faces. In Phil 1:12-18 the apostle shows his awareness that there are those whose motives for preaching the gospel are less than admirable. Phil 1:19-26 deals with a more personal question: these verses suggest Paul's anxiety about his precarious position. Facing him are the alternatives of death and freedom. Paul admits that, given the choice, he frankly does not know which to prefer. In the closing section of chapter one, (vv.27-30), Paul admonishes the Philippians to lead a life worthy of the gospel whether he is with them or not, whether they continue to suffer or not ". . . so that in everything Christ is proclaimed" (1:18).

In Defense of the Gospel.
(1:12-18).

¹²I want you to know, brethren, that what has happened to me has really served to advance the gospel, ¹³so that it has become known throughout the whole praetorian guard and to all the rest that my imprisonment is for Christ; ¹⁴and most of the brethren have been made confident in the Lord because of my imprisonment, and are much more bold to speak the word of God without fear.

¹⁵Some indeed preach Christ from envy and rivalry, but others from good will. ¹⁶The latter do it out of love, knowing that I am put here for the defence of the gospel; ¹⁷the former proclaim Christ out of partisanship, not sincerely but thinking to afflict me in my imprisonment. ¹⁸What then? Only that in every way, whether in pretence or in truth, Christ is proclaimed; and in that I rejoice.

Frequently Paul begins a new section of his letters with the phrase "I want you to know . . . ," just as he begins the main message of this letter in verse 12. With the total confidence of one fully committed to providence, Paul says that even his imprisonment, an apparent set-back, serves to advance the gospel. This is so because not only the "brethren" but even the pagan guard acknowledge that his imprisonment is for Christ. Thus Christ is being preached *because* Paul is imprisoned. Further, the majority of believers have been strengthened in faith and are more courageous in their own preaching because of the testimony Paul's imprisonment represents.

Some interpreters have taken the reference to the praetorian guard as a clue that Paul was writing from Rome. But this could also refer to certain members of the guard who might have been dispatched to various colonies. The reference does not represent decisive evidence about the place of origin of this letter. Paul's vague reference to "all the rest" who heard that his imprisonment was for Christ enlarges the circle of influence, inferring that perhaps even while themselves remaining non-believers, the guards were instrumental in preaching the gospel. How often the biblical writers underscore the theological conviction that none of the forces that can be mustered in opposition to God are able to thwart God's purposes. So powerful is the word of God that even the evil powers of this world serve to confess His greatness (e.g. the Pharaoh of Egypt, King Herod at the birth of Christ, the mockers at the crucifixion, the guards at the tomb).

Paul's imprisonment affects not only outsiders (pagans, guards) but believers as well, who are strengthened. With Paul as inspiration, many grow more courageous and fearless in preaching the word and this in turn encourages Paul, giving him more cause for rejoicing. Nevertheless, despite the positive ramifications, and as if Paul's confinement were not sufficient affliction, there is an additional trial. Some "detractors," out of envy and rivalry, add to Paul's distress. Apparently they were using the occasion of

Paul's absence to malign him even while carrying on their work of preaching the gospel.

It is probably futile to try to identify this group or their precise motives for rivalry. Perhaps they had difficulties accepting Paul himself. The apostle does sometimes appear to have something of a sandpaper personality from the evidence of his many confrontations with those inside the church. Using Paul's imprisonment and his removal, how- ever temporary, from the missionary circuit to their own advantage, personal enemies may simply be relieved to have free rein to preach unhampered by their nemesis, Paul. The apostle does suggest that there is a certain maliciousness in their intent for he accuses them of insincerity and wanting to afflict him even while he is imprisoned. It is also possible that there is a rival group of Christian preachers whose motives Paul questions not because they wage a personal vendetta but because they seek some personal gain (pres- tige? popularity?) in their preaching. Paul's defense of his ministry in 2 Corinthians 10-13 carries with it the implica- tion that his preaching was less compellingly impressive than that of some whose oratory and delivery were more pleasing to the crowd (cf. 2 Cor 11:6).

In any case, at this point it is not their gospel itself that Paul denounces as he does the preaching of the Judaizers who offer "another" gospel (cf. Phil 3:2-3; Gal 1:8-9; 5:10). Here the apostle imputes to his rivals suspicious motives but concedes that, whatever their motives, Christ is being pro- claimed. Again the forces of evil—even those still lurking in people's minds—while undesirable, have no power to still the voice of God.

Strength to endure the injustice not only of his own imprisonment but of the maliciousness of the other preachers comes to Paul through his life "in Christ" (1:14). Fre- quently in Philippians, Paul will return to this theme of living and rejoicing "in the Lord" (2:19,24,29; 3:1; 4:1,4,10) or "in Christ" (1:1,13,26; 2:5; 3:14; 4:7,19,21). Both ad- versity and favorable circumstances can be faced with peaceful equanimity if one is sustained by union with

Christ. The constant is that in all things Christ is proclaimed. Also, "in the Lord" Christians support one another, giving and drawing on mutual affection. Thus Paul refers to other Christians as his children (cf. Philemon 10), his sisters (e.g., Philemon 1; Rom 16:1) and brothers (Philemon 7; 2 Thess 3:1; Phil 3:17). Union with the Lord creates a familial bond among Christians.

In opposition to those who preach from rivalry and personal ambition are those who preach Christ out of good will and love. These realize that Paul's imprisonment is "out of defense of the gospel" (1:7,16) and they share with Paul not only his gospel ministry but the trials of his imprisonment. Implicit in the dichotomy between "pretense" and "truth" in verse 18 is a warning against divisions in proclaiming the one gospel. Verse 18 holds the key to this entire first chapter and perhaps even to all of the epistle to the Philippians.

Joy

Joy is a characteristic term for this epistle, appearing twelve times and setting its general tone. Joy is found in the fact that nothing can render ineffective the preaching of Christ. Paul rejoices in this and he *will* rejoice (v.19). For Paul this is no profane mood; joy is always bound up with his work as an apostle. In Phil 1:18, joy has an ecclesiastical basis, for in all things Christ is proclaimed. The concrete form of joy is fellowship "in the Lord" (4:1). The ecclesial dimension of joy is accentuated also in 1:25 when Paul speaks of the Philippians' "joy in the faith." Joy is an essential characteristic of the relationship between the apostle and the community.

The paradoxical nature of "joy" does not detract from its real, eschatological significance. Joy is a fruit of the Spirit (Gal 5:22), opposed to the workings of the flesh. Paul's joy is not merely anticipatory nor is it dependent on pleasant circumstances as Philippians so clearly demonstrates. Joy is usually experienced in the present and nothing can make it void. Linked to hope (cf. Phil 1:19-20), joy enables the believer to bear suffering and even to face the possibility of martyrdom. Joy becomes conviction for the believer, providing the basis for the absolute optimism such as Paul expresses in Romans 8:18-19:

> I consider that the sufferings of this present time are not worth comparing with the glory that is to be revealed to us. For the creation waits with eager longing for the revealing of the children of God.

To Live Is Christ.
To Die Is Gain.
(1:19-26).

> [19]Yes, and I shall rejoice. For I know that through your prayers and the help of the Spirit of Jesus Christ this will turn out for my deliverance, [20]as it is my eager expectation and hope that I shall not be at all ashamed, but that with full courage now as always Christ will be honoured in my body, whether by life or by death. [21]For to me to live is Christ, and to die is gain. [22]If it is to be life in the flesh, that means fruitful labour for me. Yet which I shall choose I cannot tell. [23]I am hard pressed between the two. My desire is to depart and be with Christ, for that is far better. [24]But to remain in the flesh is more necessary on your account. [25]Convinced of this, I know that I shall remain and continue with you all, for your progress and joy in the faith, [26]so that in me you may have ample cause to glory in Christ Jesus, because of my coming to you again.

Paul describes his inner turmoil. Torn between wanting to die so that he will be fully united with Christ and wanting to live for the sake of his ministry, Paul wonders aloud what his own choice would be if it were left to him. Although he continues to be confident that either way, Christ is proclaimed, he expresses with characteristic *pathos* the anxiety of one whose destiny is not only uncertain, but left in the hands of enemy forces.

Paul relies on the prayers of the community and the help of the Spirit of Christ. It is typical of Paul to ask for prayers (Rom 15:30; 2 Cor 1:11; 1 Thess 5:25), aware as he is that a thorn in his flesh (2 Cor 12:7) prevents him from becoming proud. The kind of help Paul expects from the Holy Spirit is not known—probably Paul himself did not know what to pray for (see Rom 8:26); nevertheless, Paul is confident that he will be helped and he will be saved. Nor are we certain whether Paul speaks of deliverance from imprisonment and vindication of the accusations against him (as 1:25-26 seems to indicate) or whether his confidence is rooted solely in final salvation since verses 20-21 suggest death is an actual, imminent possibility.

The prayers of the community and reliance on the Spirit prohibit Paul from excessive worry about his future. Implicitly he puts his trust in the promise of Jesus that the Spirit will come to the aid of Christians when they are arrested and brought before court (cf. Mk 13:11; Mt 10:19-22; Lk 12:11-12). This confidence allays Paul's fears and strengthens him with the assurance that he will "not be ashamed" anymore than he is ashamed of the gospel (cf. Rom 1:16). Either possibility, be it life or death, serves to the glory of Christ.

Verses 21-22 are very familiar and have received a variety of interpretations. Paul conceives his whole life as a glorification of Christ. If by dying he glorifies Christ, this is "gain" in so far as the glorification of Christ is the purpose of Paul's entire existence. Paul is not thinking of receiving a reward after death but his one preoccupying thought is the promotion of the gospel. Again the idea of 1:18: whether in life or death, Christ may be proclaimed!

Yet as profound as Paul's confidence is, his vocabulary, broken syntax and the vividness of his description betray a turbulence that is hardly superficial. Echoed here are the profound sentiments of the synoptic presentation of Jesus in the Garden. The Christian facing death realizes all too well that this is not a time for pious platitudes. The moment of death is the ultimate test of faith. And even if fear is overcome so that death seems welcome, the Christian needs still to be alert. Paul's expressed desire for death carries with it an implicit admonition to Christians that even longing for union with God has to be subject to the will of God. Paul's own desire to be "with Christ" must be subordinated to his pastoral responsibilities. So Christians, too, must accept the obligations to one another for the building up of the church until the time when their union with Christ is to be completed.

Almost as if Paul's meditation on death is interrupted, verses 25-26 break in with renewed, energetic confidence. Paul will not indicate anxiety about his future again until 2:19-27. Completely the pastor, it is as if Paul reminded himself of his ministry and shook off thoughts of preferences about his immediate fate. His ministry among the Philippians is unfinished. The community there would be much aggrieved by his death. The only important point is seeking the glory of Christ in the extension of the gospel. Thus Paul dispels his anxiety. The advancement of the gospel (1:12) includes the Philippians' own progress and joy in the faith (1:25).

Paul puts himself before the Philippians as an example of one who continues to progress (1:26 cf. 3:12). That Paul dares to present himself as a model for others (cf. 3:17; 4:9; 1 Cor 7:8; 11:1) seems almost shocking in its presumption. Yet this would not be understanding Paul who so often warns against prideful boasting. Reflecting deeper, what pastor would dare lay out his whole life before his flock except one with an amazingly transparent humility? One who had absolutely nothing to hide, to hold back. Not arrogance but complete simplicity motivates Paul to invite other Christians to examine his life, for he himself has modelled it on Christ (1 Cor 11:1).

So sure is Paul that his ministry will literally keep him alive that he promises to come again to visit the Philippians. This is not time for empty promises. The assurance with which Paul speaks provides great comfort although the same promise made to Philemon (v.22) might have been met with mixed reaction due to the moral dilemma Philemon is found with. At Paul's *parousia*, his return, to the Philippians, they will have cause to give glory to God for the mercy shown to both apostle and community. If, in fact, the apostle did write from confinement in Ephesus, the allusion in Acts 20:1-6 to a return visit to Philippi could indicate that Paul kept his word. But this remains more of a conjecture than a certainty.

Lead A Life Worth Of The Gospel.
(1:27-30).

> [27]Only let your manner of life be worthy of the gospel of Christ, so that whether I come and see you or am absent, I may hear of you that you stand firm in one spirit, with one mind striving side by side for the faith of the gospel, [28]and not frightened in anything by your opponents. This is a clear omen to them of their destruction, but of your salvation, and that from God. [29]For it has been granted to you that for the sake of Christ you should not only believe in him but also suffer for his sake, [30]engaged in the same conflict which you saw and now hear to be mine.

Philippians 1:27-30 provides a transition. This passage might seem to belong more naturally with the second chapter than with the preceding. Paul calls on the Philippians to "lead a life worthy of the gospel." Such a life is further described in chapter two as "being in full accord and of one mind" (2:2), putting on the mind of Christ Jesus (cf. 2:5). But our section can also be linked to the key idea of 1:18 which, paraphrased, insists that no matter what happens, in all things Christ is proclaimed. In 1:12-18, Paul spoke of the various reactions of believers and non-believers to his imprisonment and of the differences between those who preach in pretense and those who preach in truth. In

1:19-26, he expressed his own inner turmoil and anxiety about his fate. Now in 1:27-30 he turns to the problems of the Philippian community beleaguered by opponents from the outside.

The exact identity of these outside adversaries is impossible to name. The most we can gather is that the Philippians were beset by opponents they feared. In putting their minds to rest, Paul warns against fear while assuring the Philippians that the very fact their adversaries oppose the community marks them for destruction.

The passage begins with an emphatic "only" connoting the single mindedness with which the Philippians' lifestyle must mirror the gospel. The call for unity is repeated: the Philippians are to stand firm "with one mind . . . side by side . . . engaged in the same conflict" which is also Paul's. The militaristic language conjures up a battle scene with the Philippians valiantly engaged in a completely united front. They are not only to be animated by the same spirit (*pneuma*) but they are to be of the same mind (*psyche*). Divisions are intolerable in a church beset by threatening troubles from the outside. As the epistle proceeds, the impression becomes stronger that the community at Philippi was not without serious internal factions. Nevertheless, by positive reinforcement, the apostle admonishes them to remember their common faith and to be reconciled in mutual love.

"Perfect love casts out fear" (1 Jn 4:18). The gospels testify that the early Christians evidently never tired of recalling the times Jesus dispelled their fears (e.g. Mk 4:35-41; Lk 13:17; Mt 17:7; Jn 6:20). The apostle warns the Philippians against fearing their enemies. God is the judge deciding who is to be destroyed and who saved. Salvation is the goal of believers. Destruction is the end of those who oppose the believers. Hope in salvation sustains believers through the times of trial. Although persecution puts a strain on faith, Paul comforts the Philippians by reminding them that they are engaged in the same struggle that he is. More, this struggle is part of God's plan and it, too, like everything that happens is "for the sake of Christ" (v.29). Once again, even those destined for destruction are, however inadvertently, instruments for the preaching of the gospel. The conflict is neither an accident nor a punishment from God but a means by which Christ is becoming known.

Alongside his warning against fear Paul posits reality: almost the promise of suffering. All this has been "granted" (a term akin to *charis* = grace) so that you may "not only believe . . . but also suffer." Paul's words echo Jesus' invitation to discipleship accompanied as it is with a *blessing* in the Sermon on the Mount: "Blessed are you when men revile you and persecute you and utter all kinds of evil against you falsely on my account. Rejoice and be glad, for your reward is great in heaven, for so men persecuted the prophets who were before you" (Mt 5:11-12). Even while Christians are encouraged to "fear not," they are reminded that they will not, indeed, *should* not "fit" too comfortably in this world. Paul says that in his suffering he is filling up what is lacking in the suffering of Christ (Col 1:24). And Christ also identifies with the suffering of believers as is clear in the conversion experience of Paul who, after persecuting the church, was told by a heavenly voice "I am Jesus of Nazareth whom you are persecuting" (Acts 9:4-5).

COMPLETE MY JOY BY BEING
OF THE SAME MIND.
(2:1-4).

> **2** So if there is any encouragement in Christ, any incentive of love, any participation in the Spirit, any affection and sympathy, [2]complete my joy by being of the same mind, having the same love, being in full accord and of one mind. [3]Do nothing from selfishness or conceit, but in humility count others better than yourselves. [4]Let each of you look not only to his own interests, but also to the interests of others.

Having considered some of the circumstances presently affecting the Philippians, Paul now turns to exhortation. He appeals to the community with a rich variety of terms reminding them of their common vocation. By saying, "So if there is any encouragement in Christ," he is not implying a lack of conviction that there is. Rather he is being emphatic, insisting that *since* there is encouragement "in Christ," (see above comment on 1:14) and since all believers hold fast to Christ, then mutual encouragement, incentive, community and affection necessarily follow.

The *RSV* translation of Paul's five-fold appeal does not seem quite strong enough. Rather than mere "encouragement" (*paraklesis*) Paul means something more cogent such as "exhortation" or "urging," as he says in 2 Cor 5:14: "the charity of God *compels* us." The Greek word translated "incentive" (*paramythion*) conveys this sense of urgency. The word "participation" translates the Greek *koinonia* which might be better rendered "community" as long as we remember that, for Paul, community is not a closed group but is grounded in a sharing of common faith (see above comment on 1:5). More than "affection" is involved in the Greek *splagchna*; this term refers to the seat of all emotion, particularly love. The fifth and last appeal is to sympathy (*oiktirmoi*) signifying "deep compassion."

Paul makes his appeal in strong, ardent language, not only pleading that the Philippians will be reconciled among themselves, but demonstrating the depth of his own pastoral concern. Verse 2 indicates how strengthened the community will be if Paul's appeal is heeded. The Greek verb *phronein* is used twice in this verse and connotes having harmony of mind or agreeing with one another. The eight times this term occurs in Philippians is an indication of how important Paul regards the reciprocal concern it conveys. In Rom 14:6, the RSV translates the same verb as "honor," a rendering that catches something of the mutual respect necessary to achieve harmony in thinking as well as in daily living.

The repetition of near synonyms, all describing aspects of unity is decidedly intentional. Paul is convinced of the power of positive thinking. If the Philippians concentrate on unity, their disagreements will disappear. Again in 4:4-9, the apostle will put before his readers ideals they should reflect on in order to enliven community. When the Philippians have developed greater unity, Paul's own joy will be complete (cf. Jn 16:24; 17:13; 1 Jn 1:4; 2 Jn 12). Already Paul indicated that he could be joyous even when imprisoned, even when persecuted. But as firm as his joy is already, and as full of affection for the Philippians as he is, he will only be satisfied when they have achieved greater solidarity. The pastor participates in the experiences of his communities. When they are joyous, he rejoices. When they have difficulties, he agonizes. In the words of Paul himself, he is in labor pains until Christ is formed in them (cf. Gal 4:19).

The root of their problem is in their "petty deceits" and self-seeking (v.3). The antidote is meekness; that is, recognition of one's dependence on God. This induces humility with one another. Humility was not a virtue in the Greek world where it was portrayed as a sign of weakness. Only in the New Testament teachings of Jesus and the apostles is it featured as the key to greatness in the kingdom of God (e.g. Mk 9:35; Mt 18:1-4; Lk 10:21-24; Rom 12:3). Paul adds gentleness to the Stoic lists of virtues he borrows (e.g. Gal 5:23), extolling its implications to the point where, because it is an essential expression of charity, it is right at the heart of Christian faith.

Humility will enable Christians to recognize and emulate the virtues of others. In verse 4 Paul is advocating not so much disregard for one's own "interests" as positive recognition of each *other's* gifts. It is the same idea as he develops in 1 Cor 12-14 where, by placing the hymn of charity (1 Cor 13) between two chapters that discuss the use of the gifts of members of the community, Paul challenges all to appreciate the others. This is the opposite of causing friction and dissension. Having admonished the Philippians to concentrate on unity and on the gifts of one another, Paul has prepared them to take Christ as their model (Phil 2:5-11).

HAVE THIS MIND AMONG YOURSELVES, WHICH WAS IN CHRIST JESUS.
(2:5-11).

> [5]Have this mind among yourselves, which was in Christ Jesus, [6]who, though he was in the form of God, did not count equality with God a thing to be grasped, [7]but emptied himself, taking the form of a servant, being born in the likeness of men. [8]And being found in human form he humbled himself and became obedient unto death, even death on a cross. [9]Therefore God has highly exalted him and bestowed on him the name which is above every name, [10]that at the name of Jesus every knee should bow, in heaven, and on earth and under the earth, [11]and every tongue confess that Jesus Christ is Lord, to the glory of God the Father.

Paul interrupts his exhortations to the Philippians with a Christological hymn (verses 5-11) that probably predates the apostle himself. This is a hymn he found especially apt to communicate his message. Comparable Christological hymns can be found in 1 Tim 3:16; Col 1:15-20; Heb 1:3-4; Jn 1:3-4; Jn 1:1-14; 1 Pet 1:19-21; 2:21-25; 3:18-22. In general, these Christological hymns refer to Christ's pre-existence, incarnation, and exaltation. The style and language and especially the Christology of Phil 2:5-11 have prompted interpreters to question Paul's authorship. It seems that he had a ready-made hymn whose rhythmic style and language reflect a liturgical origin. Interested in grounding the ethical considerations of 1:11-2:4 in Christology, Paul quotes this hymn to remind the Philippians about the meaning of Christ's death and resurrection. He is not so much placing Jesus' earthly life before their eyes as a model and certainly not as one model among many. Much more importantly, Paul is recalling the significance of Christ as saving event.

To say that 2:5-11 is pre-Pauline is not to say that it is *un*-Pauline. By portraying Christ in his pre-existence, his role as servant and his exaltation as Lord, Paul is underscoring the cosmic significance of God's saving deed in Christ. Having been "in the form of God" (v.6), Jesus "emptied himself" (v.7) to the point of becoming a servant and then, after dying an ignominious death, He was "exalted" by God (v.9) to receive the homage of all creation (v.10).

Many interpretations have been given to these verses making the literature on them legion. We shall restrict our comments to identifying some of the more obvious Old Testament influences especially as they affect Paul's Christology developed here and elsewhere in indisputably authentically Pauline passages. This is done in the hope that Christology will provide the key for understanding why the apostle chose this liturgical hymn to help motivate the Philippians to work toward greater unity. After looking at the Old Testament background of Pauline Christology, we will draw some conclusions about the universal, cosmological ramifications of Paul's doctrine of redemption.

The Old Testament Background for Phil 2:5-11

Some interpreters, especially those that emphasize the need to demythologize the New Testament, trace the Christological background of this hymn to a Hellenistic or gnostic notion of a "heavenly man" who descended to earth to carry out his redemptive mission. But it does not seem necessary to go so far afield in order to locate the origin of the "emptying-exaltation" motif present in this passage. Nor does it seem necessary to accept an exclusively Hellenistic explanation for Paul's thought.

Standing at the junction where two religious traditions intersected, Paul denies that we must submit to the disorderly spirits who are hostile and threatening, as the Greeks thought. On the other hand, he affirms that there is a divine purpose in the working out of history, as the Jews hoped. The Hellenistic tradition emphasized liberation from spiritual forces of all kinds. Paul expresses his conviction that even the mighty spirits bow down and recognize that the obedient Christ is the Lord of all created beings, even of the spirits themselves. The Judaic tradition would be more inclined to emphasize liberation from sin, guilt and death. This is the freedom the Jews looked for in the law but which Paul says is found rather in Jesus.

Thus, in addition to possible Hellenistic influence, several Old Testament images provide a rich background that could have and probably did inspire the early Christian imagination to speak about Christ's emptying of Himself and His exaltation: specifically these images include Adam, Isaiah's Servant of the Lord, Daniel's Son of Man, and Wisdom. We can briefly capsulize Paul's use of these images.

According to the apostle, Adam is the antitype, the opposite of Christ. But he is still a "type," a point of comparison. By one man (Adam) sin entered the world; how much more powerful, Paul argues, is the saving influence of Christ who brought grace into the world (Rom 5:12-21). If in our humanity, we bear the image of Adam, how much more firm is our expectation that we shall image the Lord. As Paul says, extending the comparison between Christ and Adam in 1 Cor 15:45-49: "As it is written, 'The first man Adam became a living being'; the last Adam became a life-giving spirit. The first man was from the earth, a man of dust; the second man is from heaven. As was the man of dust, so are those who are of dust; and as is the man of heaven, so are those who are of heaven. Just as we have borne the image of the man of dust, we shall also bear the image of the man of heaven." Thus, in key passages in

Romans and 1 Corinthians, Paul reaches for Adam imagery to describe the universal effects of Christ's redeeming act.

In addition to Adam, the Old Testament supplied the image of the Servant of the Lord which the apostle finds particularly fitting to describe the mission of Jesus. Is 52-53 speaks of the Servant as one who bore the sins of many and thus brought about the righteousness of many. Isaiah says, "He makes himself an offering for sin . . . the righteous one, my servant, shall make many to be accounted righteous" (Is 53:10-11). Paul's doctrine of justification reflects the image of the Suffering Servant of Isaiah. Contrasting the claims of the law with the promises of Christ, Paul says in Rom 3:21-24: "No human being will be justified in his (God's) sight by works of the law, since through the law comes knowledge of sin. But now the righteousness of God has been manifested apart from the law, although the law and prophets bear witness to it, the righteousness of God through faith in Jesus Christ for all who believe . . . they are justified by his grace as a gift, through the redemption which is in Christ Jesus, whom God put forward as an expiation by his blood . . . ."

Another Old Testament image that provides the backdrop for Paul's and other early Christian writers' interpretation of the saving work of Christ is that of the son of man depicted in Dan 7:13-14: "I saw in the night visions and behold, with the clouds of heaven there came one like a son of man and he came to the Ancient of Days. And to him was given dominion and glory and kingdom, that all peoples, nations and languages should serve him; his dominion is an everlasting dominion which shall not pass away, and his kingdom one that shall not be destroyed."

The son of man is pictured as ascending to the heavens to receive authority and dominion. Then he descends to the earth to exercise authority and to restore the earth to the Ancient of Days. Paul reflects comparable ideas in 2 Cor 10:5 where he says, "We destroy arguments and every proud obstacle to the knowledge of God, and take every thought captive to obey Christ."

The ascent-descent motif is found in one of the most important passages of Paul; namely, Rom 10:6-8, itself a running commentary (=*midrash*) on Deut 30:12-14. In Rom 10:6-8, Paul employs Deut 30:12-14 as a "proof text" for his statement in Rom 10:4 that "Christ is the end of the law." The law has already been fulfilled by Christ in its soteriological sense (i.e., its intention to provide a means of salvation); and thus the law is terminated in the ethical sense of making demands (i.e., as a necessity). Believers need no longer ask: "Who will ascend to the heavens to bring down the revelation of God's will?" (Deut 30:12; cf. Rom 10:6). Nor should they query, "Who will descend into the abyss?" Paul adapts Moses' question: "Who will cross over the sea?" (cf. Deut 30:13; Rom 10:7). For, as Paul, drawing on Moses, says, "The word is near you (Deut 30:14) . . . that is the word of faith that we preach" (Rom 10:8).

Like Daniel's son of man, Christ is commissioned to restore all to God, as Paul says in 1 Cor 15:24-25: "Then comes the end when he (=Christ) delivers the kingdom to God the Father after destroying every rule and every authority and power. For he must reign until he has put all his enemies under his feet."

The likeness to the son of man is only implicit; yet it did influence Paul's use of this liturgical hymn in Philippians.

The wisdom literature of the Old Testament furnishes another concept that could have inspired Paul and other New Testament writers as they developed their Christologies. Wisdom is pre-existent, already present and participating in the creation of the world (cf. Wis 9:9). Wisdom has to be *revealed*; one cannot attain wisdom through human study or discernment. Wisdom is God's gift. It empowers humans to acknowledge God's work in creation and especially in redemption (Wis 7:15-21; Rom 1:20). Paraphrasing a passage from Wisdom, Paul asks rhetorically in Rom 11:34-36: "For who has known the mind of the Lord or who has been His counsellor? Or who has given a gift to Him that he might be repaid? For from Him and through Him and to Him are all things . . ." (cf. Wis 9:13).

God dispatches wisdom from the heavens; He sends her down from above.

A key to Paul's Christology is his identification of Christ with wisdom. The hymn of Philippians celebrates the pre-existence of Christ who freely gave of himself. The universe is not alien and hostile. All things are ordered for fulfillment in Christ through whom, as Paul asserts in 1 Cor 8:6, all things come and through whom we go. Like wisdom, Christ has come down to us as gift. He has revealed God to us and his mission is to restore all to God. These and other characteristics of wisdom influenced Paul's recourse to this Christological hymn that pictures Christ's "emptying" himself and then being exalted. Further discussion of Phil 2:5-11 will be limited to this dynamic in Pauline Christology.

Christ "emptied" himself

Attributing to Jesus the title "slave" (*doulos*), Paul expresses the extent of Christ's "emptying" (*kenosis*). The term "slave" contrasts drastically with being in "the form of God" and with the *kyrios* (=Lord) title that Jesus receives at the end of the passage. When Jesus emptied himself, taking the form of a slave, he went even further than giving us a model on which we can pattern a new attitude; the term "slave" denotes a whole new mode of existence. Paul's purpose is no longer exhortation but kerygmatic; i.e., he proclaims the message of the cross. This is the essential proclamation. It is folly for the Greeks and scandal for the Jews (cf. 1 Cor 1:23). Christ's servanthood, which is the meaning of the cross, is the very reason the gospel is rejected. by taking on the form of a servant and becoming obedient even to death on the cross, Jesus reveals how complete is his participation in humanity.

The gospels have much to teach us about the centrality of the message of the cross. Jesus' own journey to Jerusalem, in obedience to God, was punctuated with predictions of the Passion and instructions on Christian greatness. Mk 10:45 provides a key to the entire gospel preaching: "The

Son of Man came not to be served but to serve and to give his life in ransom for the many." While the disciples actively struggled against the implications of such teaching, Jesus called them again and again to fidelity to the cross. John's presentation of Jesus washing the disciples' feet is only really understood in all its poignancy when it is remembered that this was the duty of a slave and non-Jewish slaves at that. Jesus humbled himself to perform a service that was not even expected of the disciples for their Master.

The humiliated and suffering servant was not a popular Jewish image for the Messiah. The servant was described as one without beauty, despised and rejected, a man of sorrows, familiar with suffering (Is 53:2-3). Yet Christians chose this and passages like Ps 22 ("My God, why have you forsaken me?") to express the message of the cross and the extent of Christ's sacrifice "for the justification of many" (Is 53:11).

Paul's intention is more than hortatory although in Jesus Christians have a model after which they can form a new mind. Only when they have been *transformed* by the servant mentality of Christ will Christians achieve the mutuality of love and respect that should characterize relationships within their communities. Jesus provides more than an example; his saving act on the cross em-powered the disciples to imitate him in their relationships with one another.

Just as there is in Christ the "form" or image of God (cf. 2 Cor 4:4), so Christians are called to assume the image of Christ (cf. 2 Cor 3:18). This image must become increasingly more evident in believers who are being fashioned according to the mind of Christ (cf. Phil 2:5; 1 Cor 2:16; Rom 15:5). "Mind" in this context refers to more than intellect; it is the essential character whereby Christ freely gave himself to the will of God by accepting the redeeming death on the cross.

God Exalted Him

Jesus' act of obedience was crowned when the Father raised him from the dead, elevating him to a place of honor.

The resurrection is God's response to the obedience represented in the crucifixion. But not only does God raise Jesus from the dead, He exalts him, giving him a name that surpasses all others. Because he suffered humiliation, Jesus is now raised up to equality with God. He renounced equality as his inherent right and privilege. Only after redeeming the world through the incarnation does Jesus claim the homage of every bowed knee and the confession of every mouth. The hymn emphasizes universality. Jesus' Lordship is to be recognized by all that is in heaven, on earth or under the earth. Neither height nor depth nor anything can hinder this Lordship (cf. Rom 8:39); all that exists is to be brought into the captivity of obedience to Christ who is reconciling all to God (2 Cor 10:5; Rom 5:1).

The name Jesus is given which is above all other names is kyrios (=Lord). Jesus' Lordship is related to his resurrection and exaltation; it is contrasted with the title "slave" he assumed by the incarnation and crucifixion. The fact that Jesus is confessed as *kyrios* is to the glory of God who raised him from the dead (cf. Rom 10:9). Belief in the resurrection and confession of Jesus' Lordship are interrelated. The relation between resurrection and Lordship is also expressed in Mt 28:18 in the saying of the Risen Lord: "And Jesus came and said to them, 'All authority in heaven and on earth has been given to me.'"

In the context of our hymn, the title *kyrios* appears as an acclamation. Spiritual as well as human powers acknowledge the homage due to the enthroned Lord. "Jesus is Lord" counts among the earliest Christian confession formulations. Named Lord by the resurrection, Jesus now reigns over all until the consummation of the world when all will appear before His judgment seat (cf. 2 Cor 5:10). Although it is cosmic in scope, the Lordship of Jesus is centered primarily on his Lordship over people. This emphasis suggests an original baptismal setting for this hymn.

Christ effected universal access to salvation. As cosmic Lord, Christ will restore all things to God. Exhalted as *kyrios*, he will bring all things under obedience (cf. 2 Cor 5:10; Phil 3:21). The universal, cosmic effect of Christ's redemption is celebrated in the hymn of Col 1:15-20: "He is the image of the invisible God, the first born of all creation; for in him all things were created, in heaven and on earth, visible and invisible, whether thrones or dominions or principalities or authorities – all things were created through him and for him. He is before all things and in him all things hold together. He is the head of the body, the church; he is the beginning, the first born from the dead, that in everything he might be pre-eminent. For in him all the fullness of God was pleased to dwell, and through him to reconcile to himself all things, whether on earth or in heaven, making peace by the blood of his cross." And again in 1 Tim 3:16: "Great indeed, we confess, is the mystery of our religion. He was manifested in the flesh, vindicated in the Spirit, seen by angels, preached among the nations, believed in the world, taken up in glory."

Similarly, the author of Hebrews says, "He reflects the glory of God and bears the very stamp of his nature, upholding the universe by his word of power. When he had made purification for sins, he sat down at the right hand of the Majesty on high, having become as much superior to angels as the name he has obtained is more excellent than theirs" (Heb 1:3-4).

The pattern of Jesus' mission was that of humiliation-exaltation, based on the portrayal of the wise, righteous one of wisdom literature (cf. Wis 18:14-25; Ecclus 24:1-47). There are remarkable parallels between wisdom embodied in the obedient just one of later Judaism and the vindicated and exalted Christ. The connection could have been due to the new possibilities that were opened up thanks to the Hellenistic Jewish mission. Such convergence seems all the more appropriate when it is remembered that the hymn probably originally had a baptismal setting.

There are primarily three elements that point to a baptismal liturgy as the original setting for this hymn: 1) the

confession of faith based on the resurrection, 2) the prominence of the name of Jesus who is Lord and 3) conformity
to the likeness of Jesus who himself was in the form of God.
In the experience of the early Christians, baptism provides
the space where soteriology and ethics converge. The motivation for Christ's action as well as for the commitment
of those who follow him is freedom. Freedom is conceived
as liberation from a hostile and alien world, from evil
spirits, from death, the law, sin. The relevance of the hymn
is its response to some of the timeless questions that haunted
people of the first century and still bother people today;
questions such as, "Are we at the mercy of foreign, spiritual
powers in the world"? "No," says Paul, "since we have a
Lord who is above all others." "Is God indifferent to us?"
God does care about us; there is a salvation plan being
worked out in history. We are empowered to image God in
the world. The hymn is complete. With it, Paul has given his
ethics a Christological underpinning. He turns again to the
situation in the community of Philippi.

GOD IS AT WORK IN YOU.
(2:12-18).

> [12]Therefore, my beloved, as you have always obeyed, so
> now, not only as in my presence but much more in my
> absence, work out your own salvation with fear and trem-
> bling; [13]for God is at work in you, both to will and to work
> for his good pleasure.
>
> [14]Do all things without grumbling or questioning, [15]that
> you may be blameless and innocent, children of God with-
> out blemish in the midst of a crooked and perverse genera-
> tion, among whom you shine a lights in the world, [16]hold-
> ing fast the word of life, so that in the day of Christ I may
> be proud that I did not run in vain or labour in vain.
> [17]Even if I am to be poured as a libation upon the sacri-
> ficial offering of your faith, I am glad and rejoice with you
> all. [18]Likewise you also should be glad and rejoice with me.

Having quoted a hymn to remind the Philippians of the saving act of God in Christ already at work in their midst, Paul turns again to the community whom he addresses as "My beloved." He resumes the urging, pastoral style that preceded 2:5. Paul reminds his friends at Philippi that this initial obedience has to continue. Within the New Testament, "obedience" is a markedly Pauline word (Rom 6:17; 16:19; 2 Cor 7:15; 10:6; 2 Thess 3:4; Philemon 21), occurring only five times in all the gospels (Mk 1:27; 4:41; Mt 8:27; Lk 8:25; 17:6). The word obedience has its root in the term "hearing." Paul coins the phrase the "obedience of faith" (Rom 1:5; 16:26; cf. "hearing of faith," Gal 3:2,5) by which he expresses the openness to God's will that faith requires. Paul begs the Philippians to remain open (difficult to do in the light of some of Paul's criticisms, the fact that they had enemies and internal divisions) and to obey (that is, try to unite factions), whether he was there to help them or not. While reassuring them of his love, he does not lessen its demands. Paul refers again to his tenuous future, refraining from unrealistically comforting the Philippians with unfulfillable promises to come to their aid.

The phrase "work out your salvation in fear and trembling," despite the vigorous reminder that immediately precedes it, appears abrupt and out of beat with verse 13's "God is at work in you." It may be that Paul's concept of salvation is best understood in the context of this epistle more than in any other. Salvation must be seen not so much in personal or interior terms but in corporate ones. The basic meaning of the word "salvation" is physical and refers to good health. Paul is pleading with the Philippians to develop healthy relationships within the community. "Fear and trembling" could refer to the respect due to one another that will inspire the Philippians to persevere in forming strong community (cf. 2 Cor 7:15-16). This is a godly work (v.13). The effect of salvation, understood as growth in relationships within community, is to produce a state of "good will" (*eudokia*) among the Philippians.

This "social interpretation" seems to be confirmed in Paul's admonitions against grumbling and complaining. Paul explains that internal conflicts are particularly destructive because the Philippian Christians are called to a communal witness in the "midst of a crooked and perverse generation." Echoing the thoughts of Jesus expressed in the Sermon on the Mount (Mt 5:14-16 cf. Lk 11:33), Paul reminds the Philippians that they shine as lights to the world. Their experience is a beacon to the unbelieving and disoriented. They hold out to a broken world the possibility of community. Personal talent and intelligence may be remarkable without being exceptionally Christian. But the collective witness of Christians' believing with the same faith, hoping with the same boundless hope is only made possible through the spirit (cf. 1 Cor 12-14).

The Philippians are to strive for innocence as children of God; again we are reminded of the message of Jesus who placed a child as an example before the eyes of his followers (Mk 9:36-37; Mt 19:13-15). Innocence must be sought; it is not the first state but rather the final goal of Christian life. Elsewhere Christians are exhorted to be as "simple (*akeraios*) as doves" (but as wise as serpents!; cf. Mt 10:16) and "simple (=guileless) concerning evil" (Rom 16:19).

Living in a hostile world, Christians are to be above reproach. Like Paul's, theirs must be a model life. Then the world will renounce its sinful ways and emulate the Christian way (1 Pet 3:1-2). Begotten by God, Christians hold fast the word of life they have received. Not only do they "keep the faith" but the verb "holding fast" in 2:16 may also mean "holding out an offering." While the Philippians, in the midst of persecution that frightens them, hold fast to the gospel, they are also offering hope in and to an alien world.

Like a good teacher Paul knows the value of images. He alludes to the strains of the long-distance runner (cf. 1 Cor (9:24-27; Rom 9:30-32; 2 Tim 4-7) and a woman in labor

(Gal 4:11; cf. 1 Cor 15:58), expressing sympathy for the Philippians' trial as they face opposition, yet encouraging them that their efforts will not be in vain. These parables are followed by the language of ritual sacrifice. Although the possibility of martyrdom continues to exist, the altar scene is marked with a joyous spirit that Paul invites the Philippians to share.

In speaking about being "poured out like libation," Paul vividly describes how real is the possibility of his own sacrificial death. He implies that a violent death could become an eventuality. He describes himself as a sacrifice and an offering, near synonyms used to emphasize the sacred aspect of Paul's willingness to die. This is liturgical language and Paul's "liturgy" consecrates his entire life as a "living sacrifice, holy and acceptable to God"(Rom 12:1). Indeed there is, for the Christian, no profane offering. Even the financial aid the Philippians sent Paul with Epaphroditus (4:18) is a "fragrant offering . . . holy and acceptable to God." Of how much more worth is Paul's life itself.

Again Paul speaks of the joy that sustains him. This joy is infectious. If the Philippians really understand the significance of Paul's offering, they too will rejoice. Surely if they are willing to share in the sufferings of their apostle, they will eagerly embrace his joy. As he does so often with terms, Paul adds the prefix *syn* (= together with) to the verb "rejoice" in vv.17-18. The united experience of sharing the same emotions indicates the close bond between apostle and church while it underlines the importance of the unity that overwhelms divisions.

HONOR SUCH PEOPLE:
TIMOTHY AND EPAPHRODITUS.
(2:19-30).

Paul begins to wind up chapter 2 by speaking of such limited plans for the future as he is able to make. He expresses his gratitude for his companions, Timothy and

Epaphroditus, both of whom are apparently well-known to the community. These references interrupt the flow of Paul's exhortations which will resume with more bite in chapter 3.

Timothy's Worth You Know.
(2:19-24).

> [19]I hope in the Lord Jesus to send Timothy to you soon, so that I may be cheered by news of you. [20]I have no one like him, who will be genuinely anxious for your welfare. [21]They all look after their own interests, not those of Jesus Christ. [22]But Timothy's worth you know, how as a son with a father he has served with me in the gospel. [23]I hope therefore to send him just as soon as I see how it will go with me; [24]and I trust in the Lord that shortly I myself shall come also.

Paul's hope is "in the Lord." Concretely he means to send Timothy to Philippi soon. Nowhere else in speaking about proposed trips (cf. Rom 15:24, 1 Cor 16:7; 2 Cor 13:6; 1 Tim 3:14; Philemon 22) does he couple his plans with this phrase "in the Lord." It is not so much when he is making plans but when he is plagued with uncertainty that he expresses total confidence "in the Lord" (see v.24). Nevertheless, whether planning or being dependent upon the disposition of others, Paul confides himself to Christ so that in all, God's will through him will be done (cf. 4:11-13).

Timothy is Paul's usual good-will ambassador. It would be characteristic for Paul to send him to Philippi to challenge and encourage the community to carry out his instructions. Paul realizes very well that people need a model, they need an in-the-flesh interpreter to show them how to live the gospel. It is Paul's natural inclination to reach out to comfort the Philippians lest they be overwhelmed with the difficulties of adequately responding to his words. Yet Paul is not free to go to his friends. So he considers the next best; he might send Timothy. Yet he himself needs Timothy. With optimism typical of him, Paul asserts that if he were able to send Timothy, he knows he would be heartened by Timothy's report back to him about the Philippians. With great sensitivity Paul reveals that news about his friends makes him glad. Thus, sending Timothy to Philippi would serve a double purpose. Timothy could minister to the Philippians as they struggle to heal their divisions, to resist fear of those who antagonize and persecute them, and to reform their lives according to faith in the saving event of Christ. Secondly, upon his return to Paul, the apostle assures the Philippians Timothy would bring an encouraging report of how healthy and vital the Philippian community had become. Yes, sending Timothy would help with the community and its apostle. Yet this is not what Paul will do.

Tenderly and humbly, Paul admits a certain dependence on Timothy at the same time deciding that his companion is doing even more good at Paul's side than he would as ambassador to Philippi. Paul testifies that there is "no one like him," an extraordinary compliment for Timothy. But even more, these few verses (2:19-24) betray how deeply Paul was convinced of the absolute necessity of Christian friendship. Without apology, Paul refrains from granting the Philippians the consolation of a visit from Timothy since, in his time of uncertainty and misgiving, Paul himself needs Timothy's reinforcing presence. Paul has *begotten* Timothy as a parent gives birth to a child; now the "child" is sustaining the life of the parent. When Paul has been brought through this period of uncertainty, he promises he will indeed speed Timothy on his mission to Philippi. The apostle tacks on another comforting hope— that shortly he himself will also be free to come.

Timothy is praised primarily for one of the most attractive and sensitive traits a mature Christian can possess. He is capable of being present, of being truly concerned about others' faring well. Timothy, Paul says, will really care for the Philippians just as he is truly unselfish in his support for Paul in confinement. This characteristic distinguishes Timothy from the others (v.21) who look out only for their own interests. In thus describing Timothy, Paul is providing the Philippians with a model to follow. If the Incarnation is really at the heart of Christian preaching, it must be taken seriously. One implication is that flesh and blood witness is necessary in order to make the gospel credible. Timothy and Paul lead gospel lives. Paul presents Timothy as one who incarnates the lessons of 2:1-18, showing by his life and ministry that it is possible to be as unselfish and caring as Paul exhorts Christians to become (cf. also, 1 Cor 12:25).

It seems futile to try to discover the identity of "the others" who are contrasted with Timothy. Paul probably is not accusing particular leaders either in the Philippian community nor in the church he knew in his imprisonment. Nor should we assume that this is another attack on the "superlative apostles" he rather sarcastically spoke of in 2 Cor 11:1-12:13 (see 11:5). Paul is simply remarking that of all the Christians or christian leaders around him, he appreciates most the virtue and integrity of his young companion Timothy. Paul indicates how rare it is to find the remarkable combination of qualities Timothy possesses. Despite his frail health (cf. 1 Tim 5:23), his youth (cf. 1 Tim 4:12), and his naturally diffident temperament (cf. 1 Cor 16:10), Timothy has demonstrated the strength of insight, tact, compassion and success in confronting unruly communities.

At the same time Paul's own humility in expressing admiration of and dependence on Timothy is remarkable. He is totally candid in holding Timothy up as a source of inspiration not only for the Philippians but also for himself. Those who mistakenly accuse Paul of egomania can learn from this generous, affectionate, unthreatened description of his relationship with Timothy in which he appears so vulnerable. This praise of another Christian is especially powerful when it is remembered that Paul is Timothy's "father" in Christ; Timothy was Paul's convert. Paul demonstrates over and over again, the necessity of learning from converts even while ministering to them. His own relationship with Timothy is particularly poignant. Having heard the gospel, Timothy offers himself to its service which includes forming community with all the others who believe it and preach it (see above, comment on community in 1:5).

Receive Him In The Lord With All Joy. (2:25-30).

25I have thought it necessary to send to you Epaphroditus my brother and fellow worker and fellow soldier, and your messenger and minister to my need, 26for he has been longing for you all, and has been distressed because you heard that he was ill. 27Indeed he was ill, near to death. But God had mercy on him, and not only on him but on me also, lest I should have sorrow upon sorrow. 28I am the more eager to send him, therefore, that you may rejoice at seeing him again, and that I may be less anxious. 29So receive him in the Lord with all joy; and honour such men, 30for he nearly died for the work of Christ, risking his life to complete your service to me.

Although Paul cannot send Timothy and he cannot come himself, he has decided to send Epaphroditus, probably bearing this letter, to the community. We cannot know much about Epaphroditus, only what Paul tells us. Perhaps he is the same as the Epaphras mentioned in Col 1:7; 4:12. He provides another example of the extent of Paul's pastoral concern, the loving care with which the apostle treats his fellow workers. It is evident that Paul is not only interested in "souls"; he takes seriously Epaphroditus' physical and emotional health. In his glowing recommendation of him, Paul shows just how intimately he knew Epaphroditus who is brother, fellow worker, fellow soldier, Philippian messenger and minister to Paul.

"Brother" (*adelphos*) is a common word in Paul. It is used to identify members of the community of believers. It seems Paul borrows a Greek idea indicating that one becomes kin with others who hold the same truths. For the Greeks, the highest good and the noblest ideal is wisdom.They become "friends" who share the same wisdom, a relationship even closer than familial bonds. A "brother" or "sister" is "one for whom Christ has died" (1 Cor 8:12). Paul adopts this Greek notion in order to express the essential mutual responsibility for justice that was at the heart of the religion of the Old Testament as it was grounded in tribal and familial relationships. But Paul could not presume that his Gentile audiences knew about the social obligations based on family ties that were part of the Jewish heritage. Thus he had to adopt a Greek model, "friendship" or "brotherhood," to express the Christian ethic. Charity becomes, for him, the *debt* Christians owe one another (Rom 13:8). Fellow Christians are family.

Epaphroditus is a "fellow-worker" (*synergos*) and "fellow soldier" (*systratiote*) with Paul. As fellow-worker (cf. Rom 16:3,9,21; 1 Cor 3:9; 2 Cor 1:24; 8:23; Phil 4:3; Col 4:11; 1 Thess 3:2; Philemon 1:24), Epaphroditus is an example for the Philippians of what it means to "be partakers in the gospel" (cf. 1:5; 4:3). Philippi was probably Epaphroditus' home and there, among his own, he seems to have shared with Paul the work of evangelization. One does not follow the gospel alone nor does one receive it passively. To believe is to commit oneself with others to its preaching. The designation "fellow soldier" (cf. Philemon 2) connotes the companionship of Paul and Epaphroditus in conflict, probably not only in Philippi as they struggled against hostile forces in the preaching of the gospel, but also in the present circumstances where imprisonment and serious illness are their foes. Phil 2:30

indicates the lengths to which Epaphroditus was willing to go in the service of the gospel and Paul; he risked death itself and, in fact, almost died.

Like Timothy's and Paul's, Epaphroditus' service of the gospel puts him at the service of others. He is the "messenger" (*apostolos*) of the Philippians and the "minister" (*leitourgos*) of Paul. Normally Paul uses the term "apostle" to describe a divine call but here it means a certain commission from the church at Philippi. Epaphroditus brought Paul financial aid (4:18; see 1:5) and other indications of the Philippians' concern. As this offering had the sacred character of "a sacrifice pleasing to God,"(4:18) Paul resorts to liturgical language when he adds that Epaphroditus is also "Paul's own liturgist." The profane use of this term simply refers to any public work. But because he believes that all work is holy for a Christian, Paul adds to this word a sacred dimension. Paul described himself as a liturgist working to bring about the obedience of the Gentiles (cf. Rom 15:16). But Paul's is not a synagogue or church service. His offering is the collection for the poor in Jerusalem (cf. Rom 15:27; 2 Cor 9:12). Indeed, he exhorts Christians, like himself (Phil 2:17), to offer their whole lives, their very selves (Rom 12:1-2), as a sacred offering. This is the meaning of Christian liturgy.

The fact that news of Epaphroditus' illness traveled to Philippi, no doubt saddening the Christians there, with reports returning to Epaphroditus and Paul, was a cause of sorrow for the companions in prison. Christians share one another's joy and pains. Sensitively, Paul remarks that his companion "longed for you *all*" (see 1:8), that he was burdened by great distress when he knew of the grief his illness caused his friends. In Epaphroditus, saddened by others' distress, there is another example for the Philippians of authentic selflessness. The nature of his illness is unknown but it involved a risk taken in the service of the gospel, bringing the Philippians' offering to Paul. The apostle assures the Philippians that Epaphroditus' illness, although it had been grave to the point of death, was over. God in his mercy had spared him and did not heap on Paul "sorrow upon sorrow." This phrase expresses the threatened despair of the apostle (2 Cor 1:8-10).

Finally Paul exhorts the Philippians to receive Epaphroditus "in the Lord with all joy." Numerous times Paul commends emissaries to various Christian communities, encouraging the communities to "welcome them in the Lord" (Phoebe in Rom 16:1-2; Timothy in 1 Cor 16:10-12; Titus and others in 2 Cor 8:16-24; and Onesimus in Philemon 8-14). This phrase means: "Consider such people valuable. Respect and honor them."

Hospitality is particularly significant as a kind of paradigm of Christian service in the New Testament. At the end of a list of virtues which Paul exhorts the Romans to cultivate (cf. Rom 12:1-13), hospitality appears, capping as it were, and embracing all the others. Paul chides the Corinthians for living a contradiction by participating in inhospitable Eucharistic celebrations (1 Cor 11:17-34). The many banquet scenes in the gospels (e.g. Lk 7:36-50; 10:38-42; 15:11-32; cf. Mk 6:17-29; Mt 14:13-21), the anointings (Mk 14:3-9; Mt 26:6-13), parables such as the Good Samaritan (Lk 10:29-37), actual financial backing by the women who accompanied him (Lk 8:1-3), and Jesus' own gracious example (Mk 1:32-34; Mt 9:18-31; Lk 19:1-10) are so many indications of the centrality of the virtue of hospitality as it symbolizes the very meaning of Christian life. The mission discourses (Mk 6:8-11; Mt 10:7-16; Lk 10:4-12) illustrate how serious Jesus considers an inhospitable attitude. Hospitality or the lack thereof forms the basis upon which the final judgment takes place (Mt 25:31-46).

WORSHIP GOD IN SPIRIT, AND GLORY IN CHRIST JESUS.
(3:1-21).

Paul begins chapter 3 with the word "finally" as if to herald the conclusion of the epistle. Actually this chapter is a kind of digression, distinct from the rest. Its tone differs as Paul, with startling urgency and very strong language, takes up a diatribe against those who are annoying the Philippians with their clamor for circumcision. The second verse and some of the last verses (vv.18-19) attack some unknown opponents, perhaps the ones who are frightening the Philippians (1:28-30). The intervening passage (vv.3-17) consists of Paul's personal testimony. The initial (v.1) and concluding (vv.20-21) verses provide encouragement for Paul's addressees.

We Are The True Circumcision.
(3:1-3).

> **3** Finally, my brethren, rejoice in the Lord. To write the same things to you is not irksome to me, and is safe for you.
> ²Look out for the dogs, look out for the evil-workers, look out for those who mutilate the flesh. ³For we are the true circumcision, who worship God in spirit, and glory in Christ Jesus, and put no confidence in the flesh.

Chapter 3, though obviously different in message and tone from the rest of the epistle, begins with the characteristic reminder to the Philippians that they should "rejoice in the Lord." When Paul speaks of repeating "the same things" he could be referring to one or all of three possibilities: first, the need he feels to keep encouraging the Philippians to "rejoice"; secondly he continues to warn them against divisions; and, thirdly, he could be repeating a warning against Judaizers.

Having reviewed their problems and his own, and having ardently pressed them for greater solidarity and forcefulness, Paul could fear they will become despondent. The cost of discipleship is great and Paul has not mitigated the gospel's implications. Even bereft as they are of his own and Timothy's supportive presence, the Philippians cannot wallow in sadness or self-pity. In fact, sufferings are themselves a source of joy ('Rom 5:3; cf. 2 Cor 4:16-18). Paul calls the Philippians to heroic joyfulness, repeating, not yet for the last time (cf. 4:4), his admonition to be glad. Whatever aspect of their situation they find depressing, Paul contends, is less significant, less powerful than joyful confidence in Christ. This is a "safe," (i.e., a "healthy") way to think. Even if our own hearts accuse us, Paul says elsewhere, God is greater than our hearts (1 Cor 4:4; 2 Cor 1:12).

It is possible that Paul is referring to his repeated warnings about divisions in the community since he has just focused on the Philippians' need for greater cohesion. This admonition is especially weighty because the community is buffeted by outside agitators and weakened by the absence of Paul and Timothy. In view of both the ensuing caution against outside agitators (v.2) and Paul's obvious preoccupation throughout this epistle with building firm community, this reference to what needs to be repeated could easily imply one more warning against divisiveness (cf. 4:1-3).

Thirdly, since Paul has just reminded the Philippians of the very positive effect of the good pastors Timothy and Epaphroditus, the implicit *apologia* for being repetitious could refer to the dangers involved in the community's being influenced by Judaizing propaganda. Adamantly Paul opposes any "other" gospel (Gal 1:6-9; 2 Cor 11:4-6), by which he means any attempts to complement the gospel with elements of Jewish observance, especially circumcision. This protest could well fit Paul's purpose in repeating in this letter (there could have been previous letters to the Philippians and similar warnings may have been part of Paul's preaching) strong admonitions to avoid those who would change the gospel by adding to it.

Speaking with forceful language that warns against the "dogs," "evil doers" and "those who mutilate the flesh," Paul echoes sentiments expressed in some of his angriest passages (cf. Gal 5:12). These labels probably refer to one group, not three different categories of agitators. The derogatory title "dogs" could be an allusion to the Jews' appraisal of the Judaizers, who consider them to be miserable, despicable and unclean (cf. Mt 15:26; Rev 22:15). Paul asserts that the Judaizers pervert the gospel, claiming that faith in the gospel is not enough for salvation and thus denying the efficacy and immediacy of grace (Gal 1:7; 2 Cor 11:13-15). They are "evil doers," planting the seeds of suspicion against anyone who preaches the gospel of grace. Although Paul often talks reverently and respectfully about circumcision, he angrily attacks those who teach that circumcision is necessary for Gentile converts as a supplement to the gospel. To preach this is to try to nullify grace.

One of the most painful problems of the early Christian community was the fact that Israel rejected the gospel. Tensions between Jews and Christians grew as the dominant Pharisees defined Judaism in increasingly narrow terms. Meanwhile, Christianity, which felt itself spiritually spawned and nurtured by Judaism, opened its doors to the Gentiles and broke down barriers to their full entrance into the Church. On the one hand Christians felt themselves heirs to the titles of Israel (e.g., "people of God," "people of the covenant"; Christians even adopted the name Israel: cf. Gal 6:16). On the other hand Christians and Jews experienced mutual resentment.

Christians appropriated some of the titles and identities dearest to Israel. Identifying the church as the "true circumcision," Paul demonstrates the intensity of the conflict even as he gives this title a new, interior, more spiritual significance (cf. Rom 2:25-29; 9:24-26; Gal 5:2-6; 6:15; Col 2:11). True circumcision is a matter of heart. It is a question of spiritual worship (cf. Jn 4:24; Rom 8:26-27).

It is characteristic of Paul to say, "We glory (i.e., boast, exult) in Jesus" (cf. Rom 1:26; 2:16; 5:2; 1 Cor 1:31; 2 Cor 10:17). The verb "boasting" appears about thirty-five times in Paul's writings and only two other times elsewhere in the New Testament. There are two radically different kinds of boasting: one is pride which is sin (cf. Gal 6:13); the second is Christian boasting, i.e., acknowledgement that all comes from God. This second requires the humility that identifies one as subject to God's grace as it is revealed in the cross of Jesus (e.g. Gal 6:14). The origins of this idea can be traced to Jeremiah (cf. 9:23-24; cf. 1 Cor 1:31). The contrast between the two kinds of boasting is clearly expressed in Gal 6:13-14 where Paul says: "For even those who receive circumcision do not themselves keep the law, but they desire to have you circumcized that they may glory (boast) in your flesh. But far be it from me to glory except in the cross of our Lord Jesus Christ . . . ."

The source of Paul's confidence is not in the "flesh" (i.e., the natural, unconverted aspect of human life), but in what God has done through Christ. In this context "flesh" may refer to circumcision (cf. Gal 6:12-13; Eph 2:11,15) or provide a contrast with spirit (cf. Rom 2:28,29; 3:19) or both. The next few verses (3:4-8) review Paul's life "according to the flesh." There Paul denounces as rubbish all the merits and advantages accrued according to the law. Paul's use of the term "flesh" is aimed not at denigrating the body but describes the pre-converted, pre-faith state of humanity. This is clear in other contexts: 1 Cor 3:1-3, for example: "But I could not address you as spiritual people but as people of the flesh, as babes in Christ. I fed you with milk, not solid food; for you were not ready for it; and even yet you are not ready, for you are still of the flesh. For while there is jealousy and strife among you, are you not of the flesh, and behaving like ordinary people?" And again in 1 Cor 2:2; "For I decided to know nothing among you except Jesus Christ and Him crucified." Paul is rejecting the idea that anything besides faith can save and therefore "count" before God. His attack does not remain an objective, detached one, but he continues in the next passage to give personal testimony from his own life about the futility of deeds of the "flesh."

Surpassing Is The Worth Of
Knowing Christ Jesus.
(3:4-11).

> [4]Though I myself have reason for confidence in the
> flesh also.If any other man thinks he has reason for
> confidence in the flesh, I have more: [5]circumcised on
> the eighth day, of the people of Israel, of the tribe of
> Benjamin, a Hebrew born of Hebrews; as to the law a
> Pharisee, [6]as to zeal a persecutor of the church, as to
> righteousness under the law blameless. [7]But whatever
> gain I had, I counted as loss for the sake of Christ.
> [8]Indeed I count everything as loss because of the sur-
> passing worth of knowing Christ Jesus my Lord. For
> his sake I have suffered the loss of all things, and count
> them as refuse, in order that I may gain Christ [9]and be
> found in him, not having a righteousness of my own,
> based on law, but that which is through faith in Christ,
> the righteousness from God that depends on faith; [10]that I
> may know him and the power of his resurrection, and
> may share his sufferings, becoming like him in his death,
> [11]that if possible I may attain the resurrection from
> the dead.

The pivotal verse 7 succinctly expresses the point of
this section: "But whatever gain I had, I counted as loss for
the sake of Christ." The gospel reverses the values of the
world. Probably nowhere is this fact more strikingly expressed than in the beatitudes (cf. Mt 5:3-11; Lk 6:20-26).
The New Testament reveals a God of surprises who does not
reckon worth as we naturally would, but calls for transformation and a re-evaluating faith. The human temptation
is to devise a merit system by which we secure a place in the
heavenly ranks for ourselves and others. Paul examines
how this temptation was operative as a measuring rod in
his own life. From the point of view of ethnic/religious

inheritance as well as a history of personal choices, Paul computes credits. The tally sheet reads "blameless" under the law (v.6). Once again the simplicity and transparency of this ardent pastor is striking. For all to see and judge, he makes a review of his life, allowing his own personal journey with all its pain to emphasize the futility of constructing a system of self-righteousness.

If indeed anyone could successfully attain righteousness according to an established standard (in this case the Jewish law) it would be Paul. His family background is flawless. His religious practices and his education prepared him for a distinguished profession as a zealous defender of Judaism. He was not content to keep the law himself but was bent on making sure that others observed it as well. So ardent is his zeal that he became an active persecutor of the Church (cf. Gal 1:11-17; Acts 9:1-19; 22:3-16; 26:4-18). Paul can never be accused of indifference; the same missionary zeal by which he distinguished himself in his career as a Pharisee marks his life as a Christian. Converted, called, missioned, he now channels this zealous energy into spreading the gospel. But there is a difference; otherwise this would not be true conversion. Fidelity to the gospel requires that Paul's zeal be expressed in charity rather than strict adherence to law that could lead to the excesses of persecution. Not by force but by preaching, Paul seeks to win the obedience of faith (see above, comment on 2:12). At a time when tension between Jews and Christians was mounting, Paul relinquished brutal weapons while aggressively and ambitiously following his call to preach the gospel to the ends of the earth. His zeal did not weaken but it transformed him from persecutor to victim. In his own life he fleshed out the consequences of learning that charity is more important than the law, people more important than rules. There is here in the example of Paul's own life a radical critique of "religion." The voices of the prophets resonate with Paul's own experience (Amos 5:21; Micah 6:6-8). Jesus commanded that we learn the meaning of God's word in a prophetic spirit: "What I want is mercy, not sacrifice" (Mt 9:13).

One question that continues to be raised among students of Paul is whether Judaism actively persecuted the Church as early as 34-35 A.D., the traditionally accepted time of Paul's conversion. It is clear that tensions escalated to actual persecution later, at least by the time of the temple's destruction in 70 A.D. The Judaism of the pre-70 period was not monolithic; it consisted of many different factions, with the Pharisees probably being the most powerful. Pharisaic tradition would ultimately see itself in conflict with Christianity as the young church developed. Pharisaism was threatened by Christianity's liberalizing relaxation of the law's burdensome aspects and its openness to Gentiles. The witness of the gospels suggests that, although Pharisaism co-existed with other strands of Judaism that were more or less tolerated, Jesus and his followers presented a more serious problem.

Typically Paul opposes self-righteousness to real righteousness which comes only with faith. As long as misguided zeal (cf. Rom 10:2) prompts us to devise systems of self-righteousness, true justification by faith in Christ is an impossibility. Paul's example represents a challenge to willingly set aside all that we count as advantage and privilege so that like him we may gain the one advantage that matters, namely, knowledge of Christ the Lord.

To have "knowledge" is opposed to being misguided. Paul reflects an Old Testament idea which stands at the center of election theology. God "knows" Israel and true Israelites "know" God (cf. Amos 3:2; Hos 6:3; 8:2; Jer 1:5; 31:34). To know Christ is much more than knowing *about* Christ. For example, Paul must have known enough about Christ before his conversion to have understood how threatening were Jesus' teachings to Pharisaism. Only if he knew at least the rudiments to Christian teaching would he have felt compelled to resist it and even persecute the Church. But "knowing Christ" includes the affective dimension that calls for personal conviction and commitment. This "knowledge" is the "gain" for which Paul gladly relinquishes all else. This knowledge surpasses all that can be considered treasure. Knowing Christ involves receiving the power of his resurrection. This is a power that enables Christians to live according to the gospel. Through this power, Christians really can walk the extra mile, turn the other cheek, make lasting promises, give generously from the heart (cf. Mt 5:31-48). Without this power, Christian life is not possible.

Knowledge of Christ enables sharing in his sufferings. Christians conform their lives and their deaths to Christ's (cf. Rom 8:29; Gal 2:20). Christ's death effected salvation. According to Paul the cycle is death-life rather than vice-versa. By His resurrection Christ becomes the first-fruits of all who die (1 Cor 15:20). His resurrection is a promise that what happened to Him will happen to His followers. Knowing Christ involves entering into community (*koinonia*) with his sufferings. The suffering of the disciple is an extension of Jesus' suffering and death (2 Cor 4:10; Rom 8:36).

Salvation is finally gained at the resurrection from the dead. Christians are already risen with Christ and they bear the power of the risen life (cf. Gal 5:16-18). But there is also a "not yet" quality about this life. Verse 11 does not express doubt in the resurrection but uncertainty about Paul's immediate future. He seems to imply a distinction between the resurrection of the just and the final judgement of those who will not share in the blessings of the age to come (cf. Lk 20:35; 1 Thess 4:16). Perhaps this is a corrective aimed at those who said that resurrection can be reduced to the experience of rebirth at baptism (1 Cor 15:12; 2 Tim 2:18).

Christ Jesus Has Made Me His Own.
(3:12-16).

> [12]Not that I have already obtained this or am already perfect; but I press on to make it my own, because Christ

Jesus has made me his own. [13]Brethren, I do not consider that I have made it my own; but one thing I do, forgetting what lies behind and straining forward to what lies ahead, [14]I press on toward the goal for the prize of the upward call of God in Christ Jesus. [15]Let those of us who are mature be thus minded; and if in anything you are otherwise minded, God will reveal that also to you. [16]Only let us hold true to what we have attained.

Christ has literally taken possession of Paul. But the goal of the apostle's life has not yet been achieved. Paul presses on to grasp the goal because he himself has been seized. Again Paul emphasizes God's initiative, but the "already-not yet" tension mentioned in the previous section continues. Through baptism we have been justified. This is the initial step toward the goal which is salvation. Grace is not so much a "state" or "condition" but a striving, a "walking in the newness of life." (Rom 6:4; Eph 4:12; Col 1:28). Paul conveys a sense of urgency as he "presses on" to the attainment of this goal. Implied is a corrective for those who suppose that the fullness of perfection (i.e., salvation) can already be had here and now. The athletic image expressed by the verb "press on" (*dioko*) suggests an active and sincere endeavor. Accomplishment of perfection as well as a complacent quietism are equally denied. Paul repeats this disclaimer in verse 13. The initial steps to salvation have been taken in that Christ has apprehended Paul. Yet, Paul has not yet achieved his goal which is "knowledge' of Christ, total response to the upward call of God. With the staccatoed speech of one excited by the urgency of trying to make his response adequate to the call, Paul's phrases are clipped, almost curt. Pressing on, he leaves behind painful memories of the privileges of his Jewish past: his persecution of the church, his blamelessness according to the law, his natural propensity to compute merit "according to the flesh." What appears as important and essential for him now is an unflagging push forward.

Extending the image of a runner, Paul speaks of his personal straining for what lies ahead (cf. Acts 20:24; 1 Cor 9:26).

Paul pursues the prize which is knowledge of Christ. The context, however, excludes the notion of merit. Once more the apostle's simplicity in holding up his own life as a model for Christians is inspiring. He follows the call of God which is uplifting, offering maturity. The term translated "mature" by the *RSV*, literally means "perfect"; Paul says, "Let as many as are perfect think this way." In a parallel passage (Rom 12:2), Paul advises that if we think of God's mercy, we will be enlightened as to what is the will of God, the "perfect thing to do." We thus follow no less than the example of God Himself as Jesus commanded: "Be perfect as your heavenly Father is perfect . . . who makes his sun rise on the evil and the good and sends rain on the just and the unjust" (cf. Mt 5:45-48). This kind of integrity makes God's command to Abraham ("Walk before me and be perfect" Gen 17:1) seem less hopelessly impossible.

Paul returns to the differences in the community. The "perfect" will follow his example and fashion their thoughts along the lines Paul describes. The verb "to think" (*phronein*) means more than intellectual assent (cf. comment on 2:2), it implies an affective commitment. Those who do not yet think this way can be converted by God as long as they embrace God as their model of integrity. To be thus converted in mind is the work of the Spirit rather than a result of simply thinking rationally or logically. The Spirit is required to help create community since, without the Spirit, individuals' gifts as well as their needs threaten to divide. Human knowledge "puffs up," it separates and maybe even alienates (cf. 1 Cor 8:1-2). Knowledge can be the opposite of Christian charity (cf. 1 Cor 13:1-13). The stronger the community, the more open its members are to revelation. The verb "to reveal" translates Paul's Greek *apocalypsein*. With the same word Paul refers to his own conversion (Gal 1:12). The term does not connote human wisdom but divine revelation. This idea of revelation is not a contradiction with the preceding but a continuation of Paul's description of perfection.

The apostle expresses confidence that the Philippians' desire to know the truth will be fulfilled in God's revelation. In 3:16-17 he uses two complementary verbs (*stoichein* and *peripatein*), both conveying the forward movement of striving, i.e. making practical behavior correspond to mental activity. Paul is suggesting that the ethics of Christian living are not in a legal code but in living example. As limited as our human striving may be to this point, we must hold firm to what we have so far achieved.

Our Commonwealth Is In Heaven.
(3:17-21).

> [17]Brethren, join in imitating me, and mark those who so live as you have an example in us. [18]For many, of whom I have often told you and now tell you even with tears, live as enemies of the cross of Christ. [19]Their end is destruction, their god is the belly, and they glory in their shame, with minds set on earthly things. [20]But our commonwealth is in heaven, and from it we await a Saviour, the Lord Jesus Christ, [21]who will change our lowly body to be like his glorious body, by the power which enables him even to subject all things to himself.

Paul again holds up his own life as an example for the Philippians to follow. The model *par excellence* is, of course, Christ, but witnessing is also the responsibility of all Christ's followers. Practical conduct (to "so live") is expressed by a word that literally in the Greek means "to walk." There should be no dichotomy between the Christians' convictions and their activity. Our lives as believers demonstrate the extent of our influence over one another. The Philippians have a "type" (*typos*), they can follow in the person of Paul and his associates (cf. 3:14; 2:4). They are urged to scrutinize the lives of Paul and others who live like Paul.

Paul contrasts his own and his associates' lives and example to the "many" who are enemies of the cross of Christ. Paul is now driven to tears in his ardent warning about these enemies. It is difficult to establish the identity of these adversaries but they are a source of pain and anxiety for Paul. Whether they were of Gentile or Jewish origins, they were almost certainly Christians who were creating havoc. Whether Gentile-Christians or Jewish-Christians, they opposed the core of the gospel which is the cross. Enmity to the cross could mean Jewish allegiance to the law: perhaps the enemies were Judaizers such as appeared in Galatia (cf. Gal 1:6-10). On the other hand, Paul's characterization in Phil 1:19-20, accusing the "enemies" of gluttonous perversion (cf. Rom 1:19-32; 16:18) and his reference to the Stoic image of the "commonwealth," suggest a possible Gentile-Christian target. In any case, these are disgracing the name of Christianity, causing apostles and community alike agitation and unrest. Such are to be avoided.

The true Christian inheritance is described in 3:20-21. "Our" true citizenship is contrasted with "their" ways. As important as their Roman citizenship was to the Philippians, their true city is in heaven. The Christians are inwardly foreigners to this world, not specifically alien to any given state but to this world, especially to the realm of the enemies of the cross.

From heaven we expect the "Savior" of our commonwealth. In Paul's writings it is unusual to have the title Savior appear as a complement to the title "Lord" (cf. Eph 5:23; 2 Tim 1:10; Titus 1:4; 2:13; 3:6). This infrequent use of the dual title could perhaps be explained as a reaction against the pagan custom of referring to gods with the title "savior" and also to worship of the emperor. Paul may be legitimizing his use of the title here in this context that opposes the Lord Jesus Christ to worldly authorities.

The attitude of Christians' enduring trials such as the Philippians were experiencing is expectation of delivery. We look for Christ's appearing as Savior, vindicator, liberator. Salvation has a physical as well as spiritual connotation (cf. above, comment on 2:12). This can be best seen in the question of Paul's jailer at Philippi after a great earthquake opened the prison doors: the jailer, referring to his personal safety, anxiously asked "What must I do to be saved"? (Acts 16:30). Paul's and Silas' answer seems to deliberately misunderstand the jailer's question for they respond "Believe in the Lord Jesus and you will be saved and all your household" (Acts 16:31).

The purpose of the Lord's coming is further described from the perspective of human longing for restoration. Aliens in this world, Christians yearn to shed this lowly body and be fashioned in the new creation. Although for Paul the body is good, it is contrasted with the spirit to express the tension between the pull of sin and human frailty (cf. Rom 7:14-25) and gravitation toward higher realities.

The hoped-for transformation is described in 1 Cor 15:42-56. We will bear the image of the heavenly Adam (1 Cor 15:45-49). Glorified with Jesus (cf. Rom 8:17; cf. Jn 17:24), we will live unto God (Rom 6:10). The return of the Lord is imminent (cf. 1 Thess 4:15-17) so that Christians long for his coming as they strain to go forward to meet Him.

The action effecting this transformation is God's own *energia* (Eph 3:7). Christ's resurrection is both promise and first-fruits of our own. It is the supreme expression of God's saving action. By his resurrection and exaltation, Christ will subject all things to himself. Thus chapter 3 ends with a throwback to the cosmic effect of Christ's reign spoken of in chapter 2 (vv.9-11; cf. Ps 8:6; Heb 2:5-9).

STAND FIRM IN THE LORD. (4:1-3).

4 Therefore, my brethren, whom I love and long for, my joy and crown, stand firm thus in the Lord, my beloved.

²I entreat Euodia and I entreat Syntyche to agree in the Lord. ³And I ask you also, true yokefellow, help these women, for they have laboured side by side with me in the gospel together with Clement and the rest of my fellow workers, whose names are in the book of life.

Chapter 4 begins with an appeal based on the familial bonds Christians share. Paul returns to an expression of his deep personal love and affection for members of the community at Philippi. In the opening verse (4:1) he twice calls them beloved (*agapetoi*); they are longed for (cf. 1:8 where Paul expressed his ardent desire to see the Philippians), Paul's joy and his crown. As one of the themes of this letter, joy has been the constant note to which Paul returns despite his realistic awareness of all the problems facing the community. The word "crown" (*stephanos*) connotes joyous festivity and tender love. The words echo Paul's affectionate sentiments in 1 Thess 2:18-20: "Because we wanted to come to you—I Paul, again and again—but Satan hindered us. For what is our hope as joy or crowns of boasting before Our Lord Jesus at His coming? Is it not you? For you are our glory and joy." Elsewhere Paul identifies his addressees as his "letter of recommendation" (2 Cor 3:2). It would not seem to require much more evidence of the strong bond Paul tried to create between himself and his communities. His is no dispassionate ministry. He holds himself accountable to his communities and warms to their identity as a reward of his apostleship. They are encouraged to "stand firm" in union with the Lord who strengthens and sustains them.

"Be at peace among yourselves" Paul tells the Thessalonians (1 Thess 5:13; cf. Eph 4:25-32). Likewise, in Philippians he entreats Euodia and Syntyche to reconcile their differences. The apostle demonstrates the extent of his concern for the community at Philippi. No quarrels are without danger to the churches nor can Paul be indifferent to them. Naming Euodia and Syntyche suggests that they were influential leaders and that their quarrel had ecclesiastical repercussions. From the context it is clear that their leadership was as significant as Clement's. Paul knows well from personal experience the importance of confrontation and even of open disagreement (Gal 2:11-21; cf. Acts 15:12-41). But a continuing antagonism can only weaken the church and scandalize those who look for role models among their leadership. Their need to give example does not mean they must reach an objectively "correct" resolution or that they must never disagree in the first place. But the struggling church needs to see that charity is the final solution; employing the term he used at the beginning of chapter 2 to urge the community to greater unity (see *phronein*: 2:2,5; also 1:7; 3:15,19; 4:10), Paul exhorts them to respect and honor the thoughts of one another.

It is clear from Paul's writings and from his frequent mention of women that women had an outstanding role in the early church (five women are named in Rom 16 and two others are mentioned without names; cf. also 1 Cor 16:19; Philemon 1:2; 2 Tim 4:21). This was particularly true of the Philippian church, founded and maintained at Lydia's house (Acts 16:11-15,40). In his letter to this church Paul has repeatedly warned against divisiveness; only if they were significant leaders would he mention Euodia and Syntyche by name. The resolution of their conflict must have been complex—more so perhaps than settling the very important pagan question over which Paul and Peter fought so bitterly—for Paul, who seems usually to have an opinion, does not pass on a clear decision but begs both women to be reconciled by putting on the same mind. Both have struggled together with Paul for the gospel. They are both well-known to the apostle as well as to all the Philippians. They are encouraged to set the good of the church above personal interests. The community that finds salvation and guidance in the lowliness of the incarnate Lord calls out for their reconciliation. In the Lord, they are empowered to extend unconditional forgiveness to one another.

Paul urges another church leader to help them make peace between themselves. We cannot know exactly who these women were, the nature of their quarrel or the identity of the leader Paul enlists to act as intermediary. All we can gather is that Paul cared about their differences and that he expresses confidence that they will "consider one another in the Lord."

The church leader urged to act as intermediary is addressed as "yokefellow," or brother in suffering. It is possible, but not probable, that this was a proper name and that Paul exhorts him to be true to his identity, taking upon himself the "yoke" of this quarrel with its suffering. It seems clear that this is someone at Philippi, since any companion of Paul in prison would hardly be in a position to provide assistance to feuding members at Philippi. Clement is another unknown member of this Philippian community.

The "elect" are those whose names are written in the book of life (cf. Ex 32:32; Ps 69:28; 139:16; Lk 10:20; Rev 3:5; 13:8; 17:8; 20:12,15; 21:27). Service of one another may seem to be so mundane as to be passed over by the world; but whatsoever is done to the least of Christ's own provides the basis for the eschatological judgement (cf. Mt 25:31-46). What is important from the Christian perspective is that nothing of what God has given is lost (Mt 6:26-27; Jn 17:12).

REJOICE IN THE LORD ALWAYS.
(4:4-7).

> [4]Rejoice in the Lord always; again I will say, Rejoice. [5]Let all men know your forbearance. The Lord is at hand. [6]Have no anxiety about anything, but in everything by prayer and supplication with thanksgiving let your requests be made known to God. [7]And the peace of God, which passes all understanding, will keep your hearts and your minds in Christ Jesus.

After agonizing over some personal differences among members of the community, Paul returns to some general admonitions for the whole church. He repeats the command he had given in 3:1 before apparently being distracted by some agitators: "Rejoice"! This time Paul will elaborate on the theme of joy. Since the Christian rejoices "in the Lord," joy can be constant. It is not conditioned by circumstances. It does not require the absence of friction nor the externals of peace. As with the preaching of the gospel, joy must be experienced "in all things" (cf. 1:18). For emphasis, Paul repeats in 4:4 the exhortation to rejoice.

After all Paul has said, it is not likely that he is sounding empty words in his appeal for constant joy. Christians live in a hostile world which inflicts suffering and fear, if not outright persecution. Paul himself experiences conflict with this world (cf. 1:30), but he has conquered fears (1:28-30), even the fear of death (1:20-26). Jesus also warned that suffering and hostility would come and that this could be reason for joy (Mt 5:12). Suffering inserts us into a long prophetic tradition. But condemning words are reserved for those who cause innocent blood to be shed: "Woe to you scribes and Pharisees who say, 'If we had lived in the days of our fathers, we would not have taken part with them in shedding the blood of the prophets' . . . You serpents, brood of vipers, how are you to escape being sentenced to hell"? (Mt 23:30-33).

Just as Paul proposed his own life as a model for Christians, so, too, the Philippians should be able to hold up for all the world to see the example of their own fairmindedness, their own integrity and graciousness. The Greek term translated by the *RSV* as "forbearance" infrequently appears in the New Testament (1 Tim 3:3; Titus 3:2; Jas 3:17; 1 Pet 2:18 cf. Acts 2:4; 2 Cor 10:1) but it conveys an idea close to the center of the gospel. Relationships with Christians should be characterized by an unconditional readiness to forgive (cf. Mt 18:10-35). Outsiders should be impressed by the Christian refusal to retaliate in kind when attacked.

Motivation for this meekness is found in the example of Christ (2 Cor 10:1). The reality that sustains believers in the firmness of their faith is that the "Lord is at hand." The gospel preaching began with a similar proclamation: "The time is fulfilled, the Kingdom of God is at hand, repent and believe in the good news" (Mk 1:15). This "nearness" explains the necessity to keep the gospel stance of being alert, watching (Mk 13:37; 1 Thess 5:6).

In a general way, Paul again admonishes the Philippians against fear. They are persecuted and maligned. They seem to have become downcast and bickering among themselves. Their anxiety indicates a certain lack of trust. Like the disciples in the boat buffeted by the wind and waves, the Philippians tended to fear that perhaps their suffering will try them beyond the limits of their faith.

Paul, like Jesus, cautions that anxiety might interfere with true prayer (cf. Mt 6:25-34; Lk 12:22). Prayer can take diverse forms: supplication, thanksgiving, concrete requests. Nevertheless, we always address the same God who is Abba. As Father, God knows what we need even before we ask. As Luke puts it, if we who are evil know how to give our children good things, how much more will God who is good give the spirit to anyone who asks (cf. Lk 11:11-13). And if, in our weakness, we do not even know how to pray, the spirit will come to us and teach us, empowering us to say "Abba" (Rom 8:26-27; Gal 4:6). Paul conveys his absolute confidence by including thanksgiving even before naming the requests (cf. also Phil 4:6). Joyful thanksgiving best describes the constant attitude of the believer.

Peace is promised to those who pray in this way. Peace is a messianic blessing (cf. Is 11:1-11; 32:17)., rooted in God. Peace belongs to those who are harassed but who maintain faith. The peace of God surpasses all human understanding; it is a "power at work in us, able to do far more abundantly than all we ask or imagine" (cf. Eph 3:20). The peace of God will keep guard over the Philippians' hearts and minds in Christ Jesus (cf. 2 Cor 11:32; Col 3:15).

It will calm all fears, arbitrate all unruly thoughts, dispel all doubts.

AND THE GOD OF PEACE WILL BE WITH YOU. (4:8-9).

> [8]Finally, brethren, whatever is true, whatever is honourable, whatever is just, whatever is pure, whatever is lovely, whatever is gracious, if there is any excellence, if there is anything worthy of praise, think about these things. [9]What you have learned and received and heard and seen in me, do; and the God of peace will be with you.

With the peace of God keeping guard over the believer, there is freedom to concentrate on the essentials: namely that which is true, honest, just, pure, lovely, praiseworthy. Typically Paul concludes his letters with ethical exhortations. In 3:1 he seemed ready to wrap up his advice to the Philippians but then apparently got distracted when he thought about those who were agitating the community. New thoughts of peace now dominate. Peace is not simply an interim disposition but it characterizes Christian relationships and is built on the firm foundation of truth, honesty, justice. Paul advises the Philippians to let their conduct be shaped by these things, all of which they have witnessed in the apostle's own life. Paul unites his exhortation "to think" with his challenge to also "do" (v.9).

Christianity is not irrational. Faith is not opposed to reason. Based on reality, Christianity seeks to flesh out whatever is true and honest. John quotes Jesus as saying, "I am the truth" (Jn 14:6). Faithful to its Jewish heritage, Christianity also affirms whatever is just. This refers not only to relationships among people, but conceived in its broadest "religious" sense, justice for Paul indicates a right relationship with God (cf. Rom 2:13). Purity for Paul means not only sexual modesty, but the kind of moral righteousness that shows self-awareness as the temple of the Holy

Spirit. As he says in 1 Cor 6:19-20: "Do you not know that your body is a temple of the Holy Spirit within you which you have from God? You are not your own; you were bought with a price so glorify God in your body." Above all, Christians are to remember that they belong to one body, the body of Christ, the church (cf. Rom 12:4-5; 1 Cor 12:12-27).

The next two virtues reinforce the social, interpersonal dimension of Christian life. Christians are urged to reflect on and love whatever is "lovely" and "gracious." That which is lovely calls forth love. That which is gracious is held in esteem by all peoples. All that is virtuous and worthy of praise would appeal to the civic minded Philippian.

Such a list of virtues would have been familiar in the Philippians' world. Elsewhere Paul matches virtues with vices (Rom 1:20-32; Gal 5:19-21; 1 Cor 6:9-10); but having stressed the need to be without fear, it is almost as if Paul does not want to introduce any negative elements. The controlling thought is God's peace.

As he has done consistently, Paul again sets himself up as an example to the Philippians. The grace of God, acting in Paul, compels Paul to give the witness of a gospel life. By stressing again his own example, Paul shows how seriously he takes the Incarnation. Christian tradition is found not only in the teaching but also in the very lives of those who follow Jesus. Authentic discipleship offers not only the peace of God but the God of peace.

I CAN DO ALL THINGS IN HIM
WHO STRENGTHENS ME.
(4:10-20).

> [10]I rejoice in the Lord greatly that now at length you have revived your concern for me; you were indeed concerned for me, but you had no opportunity. [11]Not that I complain of want; for I have learned, in whatever state I am, to be content. [12]I know how to be abased, and I know how to abound; in any and all circumstances

I have learned the secret of facing plenty and hunger, abundance and want. ¹³I can do all things in him who strengthens me.

¹⁴Yet it was kind of you to share my trouble. ¹⁵And you Philippians yourselves know that in the beginning of the gospel, when I left Macedonia, no church entered into partnership with me in giving and receiving except you only; ¹⁶for even in Thessalonica you sent me help once and again. ¹⁷Not that I seek the gift; but I seek the fruit which increases to your credit. ¹⁸I have received full payment, and more; I am filled, having received from Epaphroditus the gifts you sent, a fragrant offering, a sacrifice acceptable and pleasing to God. ¹⁹And my God will supply every need of yours according to his riches in glory in Christ Jesus. ²⁰To our God and Father be glory for ever and ever. Amen.

With verse 10, Paul returns to the personal message he addresses specifically to the Philippians. As he has repeatedly urged them to rejoice, he himself gives them an example with his own joy. Paul perserveres with the same undauntable positive attitude he has displayed since the beginning of this letter. The cause of his joy is the Philippians' generosity. Their concern for him translates their affection into action. This concern has been constant but the Philippians lacked the opportunity, the right moment to express this concern. Paul uses a Greek verb that is a derivative of the important gospel concept *kairos*, meaning the "hour," the "pregnant moment" of Christ's sacrificial death (cf. Jn 2:4; 13:1; 17:1).

Is is not clear why the Philippians are now given the opportunity to help Paul, an opportunity they had formerly been denied. Paul testifies in 1 Cor 9 that he was self-supporting and did not receive aid from the communities he served. Nevertheless he was aware of the saying of Jesus that the "prophet is worthy of his due" (1 Cor 9:14; Mt 10:10), that the disciples deserved to be supported by the

Christian communities. Despite the fact that Paul claims this as his right, he denies that he exercised it even though the other apostles did. Perhaps the Philippians only recently had the opportunity to come to his aid because Paul was incapable of supporting himself in prison. On a previous occasion he also had accepted aid from them (cf. 4:15-16). Given the closeness of his relationship with this community he probably felt freer to accept help from them than he would have from the Corinthians by whom he was apparently unjustly accused of profiting from their donations (esp. 1 Cor 9:15-18).

Although Paul himself refuses the privilege of being supported by the churches, sharing material possessions is a very important sign for him (1 Cor 16:1-4; 2 Cor 8:1-5; Rom 15:25-28). Sharing material goods represents communion in the spirit. The collection Paul carries from the Gentiles to the famined in Jerusalem is a very important symbol of the Gentiles' full participation in the church. Since spiritual blessings are the more important, it would be incongruous for those who have material possessions not to share with those in need. In fact, Paul has no patience with the Corinthians who allow social and political differences to divide the community even at the Eucharistic celebrations (1 Cor 11:17-34).

With 4:11-13, Paul diffuses any lingering fear that he is disappointed in the Philippians. He reiterates his total satisfaction with this community. Further, he repeats his avowal that he is independent from the circumstances that would normally affect those with weaker faith. He is attached only to Christ; that is the secret of his serenity. Beside Christ everything else fades into irrelevance. Because of his union with the Lord, Paul can withstand hunger, stress, imprisonment, persecution, even the threat of death (2 Cor 11:23-33)! Like the heroine of Leon Bloy's *The Woman Who Was Poor*, Paul could say, "There is only one tragedy, and that is not to become a saint."

Thus Paul voluntarily sacrifices for the sake of the gospel. His imprisonment is freely accepted. His jailers do not control him. They cannot restrain him, so great is his freedom. Like Christ he knows how to be abased (cf. 2:8). Though abounding with spiritual gifts, he boasts of his weakness and admits he suffers a thorn in the flesh that humbles him (2 Cor 12:7-10). Whether hungry or filled, his confidence is in God to the extent that part of the revelation given to him was that God's power is perfected in human weakness (2 Cor 12:9). The equanimity with which he accepts all is living testimony that his purpose is singleminded and pure. His sentiments echo once more 1:18—"Only that in every way . . . Christ is proclaimed." Nothing disturbs his peace for he confidently acknowledges, "I can do all things in Him who strengthens me."

In verse 14, Paul resumes his thanksgiving and praise for the Philippians who share in his affliction. Like the good pastor he is, Paul again acknowledges that he receives as well as gives in his ministry. He is indebted to the Philippians. In Rom 13:8-10 he admonishes that love is the only debt Christians owe one another. He thus emphasizes the strength of Christian love. It is not only a willingness to share one's superabundance; it is more fundamental and vital. Having entered into the same believing community, Christians make a radical commitment to one another. Fidelity to the gospel means continual willingness to give as well as to receive. Fidelity to the gospel means fidelity to the church. Faith in Jesus compels faith in the community of believers.

The gospel began with this basic commitment. Paul reminds the Phlippians that they have been among the most faithful ever since they first heard the good news of salvation. This "good news" is not objective data nor for Paul is it a retelling of the story of Jesus of Nazareth. The gospel is the power of God for salvation (Rom 1:16). The beginning of the gospel is the experience of allowing it to seize one; the experience of being handed over in complete receptivity to its power (cf. Rom 6:17-18).

Paul commends the Philippians for their constant kindness, implying an exhortation to perseverance. To the

Corinthians he held up the Macedonia churches as a model of generosity (2 Cor 8:1-15). Now he personally applauds them. They have become partners in the gospel, fellow members of the community of sharing. Paul again employs the term "communion" that conveys a deep degree of intimacy as he urged in chapters 1-2. The greatest sign of the Philippians' willingness to be partners is the fact that they have shared Paul's affliction. Paul uses a technical term and one of his favorites for "affliction"; a term that denotes the tribulation that will accompany the end time (cf. Mk 13:19; 2 Thess 1:6).

The Philippians even sent help to Paul in Thessalonica more than once. 1 Thess 2:9 and 2 Thess 3:8 suggest that even the Philippians' generous gifts actually did little to alleviate Paul's need. Nevertheless, it is the symbolic meaning of this generosity, the fact that it gives the Philippians an opportunity to demonstrate their concern that is so important for the apostle. As Paul tells the Corinthians, "I do not want what you have, I only want you." (2 Cor 12:14). Paul does not seek the gift so much as he welcomes what the gift signifies; namely, communion in the faith and his own docility to the gospel implications of mutual giving and receiving. With commercial terms ("fruit," "increase," "credit": v.17), Paul expresses the idea of growth in faith. As he reminded the Romans, the righteousness of God is revealed through faith and for faith (Rom 1:17). Far from being a one time commitment, Christian life admits development, growth; baptism is but a beginning.

Continuing with terminology borrowed from the world of finance, in the first part of 4:18 Paul describes the Philippians' gift that he has fully received from their messenger (Cf. 2:25) Epaphroditus. This changes to liturgical language as Paul puts the matter of sharing material possessions back into the context of its symbolic meaning. All that the Philippians do as committed Christians, members of the same body, is part of their offering their whole lives as a sacrifice to God (cf. Rom 12:1-2). Such complete submission is the only way to discern God's will. Paul does not recognize a distinction between the sacred and the profane. A tangible, charitable offering is the holiest of sacrifices.

Two ideas innate to the Old Testament message underlie Paul's emphasis here. Judaism, like Christianity, makes social justice its core. The prophets excoriated the religious leaders, the kings as well as the priests, for neglecting the defenseless while they offered empty sacrifices in the temple (Is 1:11-17; Micah 6:8; Hosea 6:6). Jesus had a similar critique of the leaders of his day (Mk 7:1-13; Mt 9:10-13; Lk 7:36-50). Religion without justice is mockery. In the words of James: "Religion that is pure and undefiled before God and the Father is this: to visit orphans and widows in their affliction . . ." (Jas 1:27). And: "If a brother or sister is ill-clad and in lack of daily food and one of you says to them, 'Go in peace, be warmed and filled,' without giving them the things needed for the body, what does it profit? So faith by itself, if it has no works, is dead" (Jas 2:15-17).

The second Old Testament idea that probably influenced Paul's expression here is that an acceptable sacrifice gives off a sweet smell. Like the sacrifice of Abel, contrasted with that of Cain, the fragrance rises to the throne of God (Gen 4:1-16). After the flood, Noah offered such a sweet-smelling sacrifice that God regretted having cursed the earth and vowed not to do it again (Gen 8:21). The prophet-priest Ezekiel proclaims the promises of God that when he gathers the Israelites, he will welcome them as a pleasing and acceptable fragrance (Ez 20:41).

Just as the Philippians helped Paul, even to the extent of denying themselves, God in his fullness and richness will pour out his abundance on them. The context dictates that Paul envisions temporal as well as spiritual blessings that will not only supply the needs of the Philippians but come from the "depth of the riches and wisdom and knowledge of God" (cf. Rom 11:33). The Philippians have sought the kingdom of God, all else will be added to them besides, as Jesus himself promised (cf. Mt 6:33).

The doxology closing this section is a characteristic Pauline outpouring of piety and commitment to Christ as well as an extension of the idea of glory. Paul often concludes his discussion of the blessings God has bestowed with a responding prayer of praise (Rom 16:25-27). Now, having reviewed the work God has accomplished in the community at Philippi, Paul seems unable to restrain his praise and gratitude to God. He confirms this doxology with a fervent "Amen." It is fitting that God be honored for his glory and his abundant blessings. So be it.

GREET EVERY SAINT IN CHRIST JESUS. (4:21-23).

> [21]Greet every saint in Christ Jesus. The brethren who are with me greet you. [22]All the saints greet you, especially those of Caesar's household.
>
> [23]The grace of the Lord Jesus Christ be with your spirit.

Paul's letters would seem incomplete if they did not conclude with some words of personal greeting. Here he greets all the saints as he urges them to greet one another. Throughout this letter there has been a consistent emphasis on the universality of Paul's exhortations. Greeting one another as saints, holy ones, requires deep respect for the dignity of *all* the members of the community. If the Philippians recognize this dignity, the difficulties of their divisions will fade. They are admonished to greet one another as they do all things, namely, "in Christ Jesus."

Part of Paul's apostolic responsibility involved keeping the local communities in touch with one another and with the universal church. Stamped with Paul's own personality as this letter is, it is not purely personal but includes his fellow prisoners and probably too, the church located where he is writing. The brethren, indeed all the saints, join Paul in greeting the Philippians.

Paul refers to those of Caesar's household, a greeting that confirms for some interpreters the Roman origin of Philippians. But, since there were many Roman colonies outside the capital, it is possible and even probable that some Roman soldiers, authorities and/or servants were stationed far from Rome. Paul could have met some of these in captivity, especially since he previously referred to himself as a well-known prisoner (1:13). Any government building could have been called Caesar's household. This reference, then, is insufficient to destroy the hypothesis that Ephesus was the place of origin.

The concluding benediction is also characteristic of Paul (1 Thess 5:28; 2 Thess 3:18; 1 Cor 16:23; 2 Cor 13:14; Gal 6:18; Philemon 25; Rom 16:20). In his introductory salutation he wished the saints of Philippi "grace" and "peace." Having described the peace of God earlier in this chapter, he ends with a reiteration of his prayer for grace. Perhaps the benediction suggests that the epistle was intended to be read aloud at the house-meeting of the community. Gathered together they form one body and so he uses the singular "your." The consistent theme has been unity and community. Now the apostle, in parting, annexes in the form of a benediction an official reminder that unity should characterize the Philippian church.

So ends one of the most beautiful and intimate works in the New Testament. Philippians lifts the veil on Paul's life and shows us a pastor fully devoted to his churches. In Philippians we meet Paul the human being who aches for a church experiencing painful divisions, a church in need of healing and encouragement, a church like ours. Philippians speaks to anyone who takes ministry seriously. Paul inspires the pastor in us with his genuine humility and his willingness to share his own fears and doubts as well as his hopes. A sensitive and loving apostle is this committed Christian. His personality and obedience to the gospel are further revealed in our second work from his pen, the epistle to Philemon.

Philemon

AN INTRODUCTION
TO PHILEMON

THE LETTER TO *Philemon*, at first blush, might seem interesting but hardly captivating. This epistle seems to be more historically intriguing than relevant for our times. But, in fact, the opposite is the truth. Philemon demonstrates, perhaps more dramatically than any other book of the entire Bible, that "conversion" indicates real change; that commitment means a life-yes; that becoming one in Christ means that "in Christ there is neither Jew nor Greek, there is neither slave nor free, there is neither male nor female" (Gal 3:28).

Sometimes people express surprise that the short personal letter of Paul to his friend Philemon should be included in the canon of the New Testament. Alongside the more generalized writings of the other epistles and the gospels, Philemon seems to be conspicuously individualized. The letter refers to a very specific problem in the relationship between two individuals within the context of a first century social structure considered passé today.

In our times of uncertain "yes" and "no"s, when political rhetoric seems to obscure the truth, when such factors as economic and political status, sex, religious convictions determine our degree of freedom, can a little letter of some 420 words cut through all our rationalization of the *status quo*? This is a strong challenge for this little giant, the epistle to Philemon. This letter calls us to take seriously the demand (a word given initially in baptism, as promise to be lived continually) that becoming a Christian changes the entire course of one's life.

As Jesus did in the Sermon on the Mount in reference to sexual morality (cf. Mt 5:27-28), Paul placed responsibility for ethical decisions on the intent of the persons involved. Paul makes it clear that the enslavement of another Christian is wrong and that he has the authority to enforce this conviction. Yet he returns the slave Onesimus, letter of recommendation in hand, to Philemon, charging Philemon to release him. This places Philemon in an awkward position to say the least. His dilemma seems insoluble in that, humanly speaking, he would compromise the whole financial and social structure of his world if he obeys Paul.

Despite, maybe even because of, this letter's friendly tone, one can "read between the lines" and recognize the impossible bind in which the sender (Paul) places the receiver (cf. James Burtchaell's *Philemon's Problem. The Daily Dilemma of the Christian* for a clear, well-developed discussion of this dilemma). If Philemon agrees that Onesimus could or should be set free, he sacrifices all semblance of order and control of other slaves. If Philemon does not agree that Onesimus be set free, he compromises the gospel. The author makes the choice clear cut. Philemon, apparently a man of virtue and Christian conviction, cannot retain Onesimus as a slave. The former slave has become a brother in faith. A brother, like a son, cannot remain a slave (Gal 4:3-7). Philemon could exempt Onesimus from his slave-status on the following conditions:

a) that he be let go only after being severely punished for having run away in the first place (9-12) and, on top of that, having apparently stolen property or caused his "owner" some injury (18). This would entail at least a public demonstration of the fact that Philemon would brook no further instances of slaves' infiltration into the Christian ranks for the purposes of being set free.

b) that he be reprimanded, bribed and dismissed quickly in order not to attract attention to the idea that becoming a Christian could entail the privileges of freedom and self-determination.

Philemon could only retain Onesimus as his slave with the following implications:

a) that he be discredited in his own Christian conviction that baptism made all equal before God. Apparently converted by Paul, "the Apostle to the Gentiles," Philemon himself would thereby compromise his own belief that slaves were as good as free people, just as Gentiles were not to be considered second-class citizens in comparison to Jews or women in comparison to men.

b) that he subdue Onesimus by punishment and then brave the repercussions of a visit from Paul. Known neither for his short memory nor for his mitigation of the gospel, Paul promised Philemon a visit shortly (v.22) and further defied noncompliance with his wishes, reminding Philemon that he himself owed Paul a debt (v.19). Paul used further persuasive tactics saying, "Though I am bold enough in Christ to command you to do what is required, yet for love's sake I prefer to appeal to you" (v.8-9) . . . and "I write to you knowing that you will do even more than I say" (v.21).

Given the complete change of attitude demanded, it is clear that Philemon's choice cannot be made along human lines. His decision must involve the radical change of gospel conversion. Paul admonishes the Christians in Rom 12:2: "Do not be conformed to this world but be transformed by the renewal of your mind . . . ." Only with a beatitude mentality can Philemon make the right choice.

In the days of Philemon, the issue was slavery. Hardly a Christian could be found alive today that would dispute the question of out-and-out slavery. Yet there are more subtle forms of slavery: racism, sexism, the enslaving devices of the socio-economic-political machinery. Philemon stands as an unswerving challenge for us to make

Christian choices, "transformed by the renewal of your mind" (Rom 12:2; cf. Phil 2:5). As with all the letters taken from this first century period, the lessons of Philemon must be translated into lessons for our times— what else could a personal letter from one individual to another twenty centuries ago imply for us who believe that God's word is revealed in inspired works? How numerous the implications! There exists no Christian option to enslave others because of race, sex, or religion. There can be no circumventing of the rights of others. Christians cannot exercise ownership of others in any way. The God Christians address is One for all; this is a God whose relationship to us makes us kin to one another.

The epistle to Philemon presents dramatic evidence of just how seriously the Christian must take the gospel. It is of such ultimate concern that it affects everything the Christian does. Obedience to the gospel is to be a liberation experience. The gospel redresses inequalities. Philemon is a remarkably relevant epistle for our times. It provides a model against which our own relationships can be measured. As long as there are any areas in any human life that are not free, Paul and Philemon have a lesson to teach. Our task is to ponder these words and make their implications felt in our world.

GRACE TO YOU AND PEACE.
(1-3).

> [1]Paul, a prisoner for Christ Jesus, and Timothy our brother,
>
> To Philemon our beloved fellow worker [2]and Apphia our sister and Archippus our fellow soldier, and the church in your house:
>
> [3]Grace to you and peace from God our Father and the Lord Jesus Christ.

As in Philippians, Paul's first words are to identify himself and Timothy as the authors of the epistle. His self-designation once again omits his more usual title "apostle" (cf. Rom 1:1; 1 Cor 1:1; 2 Cor 1:1; Gal 1:1; Eph 1:1; Col 1:1) in favor of a close identification with Timothy ("our brother") and the mention of Paul's confinement. Although when he calls himself a prisoner (*desmios*) of Jesus Christ he could mean that he has been captivated by Christ, the consensus of interpreters list Philemon among the captivity epistles actually written from prison. More frequently (Rom 1:1; Phil 1:1) Paul uses the term *doulos* (i.e. slave) which connotes the extreme degree of his dedication to the gospel. Doubtless Paul here as elsewhere refers not only to his actual imprisonment but also to the completeness of his service to Christ.

The letter begins with a greeting not only to his friend and fellow-worker Philemon but includes a woman, Apphia, and another man, Archippus. Some have theorized that this refers to Philemon's wife and son but there is no way of verifying this conjecture. Although Paul personally challenges Philemon to make a morally upright christian decision, the collective address makes the letter more than a personal document.

Philemon is called "well-beloved" and "our fellow-worker." He collaborates with Paul in responsibility for preaching the gospel. Already in the greeting Paul sets the tone of the letter. His demands on Philemon are difficult and strong but he makes them with affection and respect. Christianity calls for the complete commitment of a changed heart and although Paul does not hesitate to show its critical implications, he approaches Philemon with forceful gentleness. Apphia and Archippus are likewise greeted with terms of endearment. They are clearly fellow-Christians. Having become "related" to Paul through her conversion, Apphia is designated "our sister" just as Phoebe is in Rom 16:1 and as Timothy is both brother and son to Paul. Although he is in bonds, Paul conjures up a battle scene when he calls Archippus "our fellow soldier" suggesting that he is in conflict with the world. Paul was no insurrectionist (cf. Rom 13); the battle he wages is a spiritual one. He shows with his life that a Christian cannot live too easily in this alien world.

Further, Paul greets all the church at Philemon's house (or Paul might be referring to Archippus' house, but since his message concerns Philemon it is his household that seems to be involved). The early Christians celebrated the Eucharist and met afterwards in homes. Perhaps Philemon was a leader in his community. By writing to him and addressing all the church at his house, Paul is adding additional weight to his message. Philemon ordinarily would have been expected to share this letter with the others. But, because of the challenge of its contents, he probably would rather have kept Paul's pastoral comments secret.

Grace and peace are Paul's usual greeting (Rom 1:7; 1 Cor 1:3; 2 Cor 1:2; Gal 1:3; Eph 1:2; Phil 1:2; Col 1:2; 1 Thess 1:1; 2 Thess 1:2). This seems to have been a Pauline creation referring to God's unmerited blessings ("grace") and the reconciliation that embraces relationships between God and all people ("peace"). Peace is the work of grace in us. God's charity (*charis*) replaces the customary "greeting" of Greek usage and the Greek word *eirene* translates the normal Hebrew greeting "shalom."

THE HEARTS OF THE SAINTS HAVE BEEN REFRESHED THROUGH YOU.
(4-7).

> [4]I thank my God when I remember you in my prayers, [5]because I hear of your love and of the faith which you have toward the Lord Jesus and all the saints, [6]and I pray that the sharing of your faith may promote the knowledge of all the good that is ours in Christ. [7]For I have derived much joy and comfort from your love, my brother, because the hearts of the saints have been refreshed through you.

All of Paul's letters, except Galatians, begins with a thanksgiving just following the initial greeting. Here in

Philemon, Paul's thanksgiving is very personal and affectionate. Paul speaks of the constant thanksgiving he renders (cf. 1 Cor 1:4-9; Phil 1:3-11; Col 1:3-14; 1 Thess 1:2-10; 2 Thess 1:3-12). Prayer, gratitude, joy are Paul's continuous companions because so deep is his union with the Lord that he draws strength and perseverance from this identity. Paul's thanksgiving is motivated by the memory of Philemon; he commends him with high praise.

The idea of faith-sharing introduced in v.6, is the main theme of the letter from which Paul will draw pastoral guidelines to help Philemon make a christian decision regarding Onesimus. Paul, Onesimus, members of Philemon's household all embrace a common faith which makes them accountable to one another. Faith is truth. Those who share faith must promote knowledge of all the blessings there are in Christ. Knowledge is a means of freedom. Thus Christians are committed to promoting the freedom of one another. The very fact that the church meets in the house of Philemon makes him responsible for giving true Christian witness. In keeping with his style in other letters, Paul first identifies the Christian as one who lives out the baptismal commitment in community and then he spells out in practical terms some of the implications of this communal responsibility.

Philemon and his household are known for their faith and love, not only toward the Lord Jesus, but also toward all the saints. The "saints" are those whom God has made at peace through the reconciliation of Jesus (cf. Rom 5:1). "Saints" refers to the community of believers. Christian love is not only vertical, but must be horizontal as well in order to be real. Philemon has been generous and vigorous in sharing his faith, thus promoting the knowledge of all the good that belongs to those who live in Christ. Paul speaks of the community (*koinonia*) of faith. Tactfully yet cogently he prepares Philemon for the appeal for Onesimus' freedom. It would be incongruous and inconsistent for one who has given such good example as a leader in the church to shirk his responsibility to a former slave become brother Christian. The hearts of the saints have been refreshed by Philemon: how can his own heart now remain cold and unrelenting? Paul himself has derived joy and comfort from Philemon's great love. How can this love now act in a binding, unfreeing way?

I PREFER TO APPEAL TO
YOU OUT OF LOVE.
(8-14).

[8]Accordingly, though I am bold enough in Christ to command you to do what is required, [9]yet for love's sake I prefer to appeal to you—I, Paul, an ambassador and now a prisoner also for Christ Jesus—[10]I appeal to you for my child, Onesimus, whose father I have become in my imprisonment. [11](Formerly he was useless to you, but now he is indeed useful to you and to me.) [12]I am sending him back to you, sending my very heart. [13]I would have been glad to keep him with me, in order that he might serve me on your behalf during my imprisonment for the gospel; [14]but I preferred to do nothing without your consent in order that your goodness might not be by compulsion but of your own free will.

Paul seems tempted to turn from persuasion to an invocation of his authority. Christian conviction has impressed on him the impossibility of condoning slavery. Never one to be unsure of his own authority and even duty to command, he defends the boldness by which he is prompted to act. Paul has defended his decisiveness on many occasions. Although he has the right to command, he opts to appeal to Philemon on the basis of love. Philemon will respect Paul's appeal because Paul has the authority of age either in the church or simply having lived a long life (cf.

Eph 6:20). The *RSV* translates *presbytes* "ambassador."
This would be consistent with Paul's identification of the
Christian vocation in 2 Cor 5:20: "So we are ambassadors
for Christ, God making his appeal through us. We beseech
you on behalf of Christ, be reconciled to God."

If Paul is an ambassador, he is also a prisoner not only
of Christ but one who is actually in captivity. Therefore
he can only carry out his mission as ambassador through
messengers. The messenger he chooses is Onesimus whom
Paul now sends to procure his own freedom. Onesimus has
become Paul's "child" in prison. With the image of a father-
son relationship, Paul speaks of the quality of christian
love by which believers are joined to one another as if they
share the same blood, the same life.

Onesimus, a common slave name, means "useful" and
in speaking about his new identity, Paul makes a play on
words. He insinuates that formerly, as a slave, Onesimus
was not really useful to Philemon, in other words, he was
not himself. As a Christian he can become "useful" for now
he is cherished. As a son to Paul and a brother to his former
master, the one-time slave has really increased his value.

Somewhat reluctantly, Paul sends Onesimus back to
Philemon. In the tradition of the remarkable friendship
between Jonathan son of Saul and David the future king
in the Old Testament, Paul calls Onesimus "his own heart"
just as Jonathan loved David as "his own soul" (I Sam
20:17). Paul hesitates because he would like Onesimus to
remain with him to comfort him during his confinement.
Yet he also wants Philemon's free permission so that his
action will not be compulsory but liberating, as he counsels
Philemon to be. Another gospel tradition is reinforced
by Paul: in contrast to the Pharisees who multiply people's
burdens but never lift a finger to free them (cf. Mt 23:4), the
disciples are commissioned to be agents of freedom, empowering others with their unlimited forgiveness (Mt
18:21-35).

RECEIVE HIM AS YOU WOULD RECEIVE ME. (15-20).

> [15]Perhaps this is why he was parted from you for a while, that you might have him back for ever, [16]no longer as a slave but more than a slave, as a beloved brother, especially to me but how much more to you, both in the flesh and in the Lord. [17]So if you consider me your partner, receive him as you would receive me. [18]If he has wronged you at all, or owes you anything, charge that to my account. [19]I, Paul, write this with my own hand, I will repay it—to say nothing of your owing me even your own self. [20]Yes, brother, I want some benefit from you in the Lord. Refresh my heart in Christ.

Paul tries to find a reason in God's salvation plan that might explain Onesimus' absence from Philemon. True to his Israelite heritage, Paul implies that nothing is done accidentally but all belongs to the wisdom of God. Divine Providence oversees what happens in human life. Onesimus was parted from Philemon so that Philemon might have him back forever. The condition of slavery only exists under the law or before one has really achieved Christian freedom. But those who have died with Christ are admitted to a new freedom: slavery and death no longer hold sway over them (cf. Rom 6:5-9).

Paul does not accuse Onesimus of running away and only discreetly and indirectly does he refer to the fugitive's cheating or stealing from his former master (v.18). Tactfully and pastorally he tries to mediate any disagreement. The basic gospel call for justice and unlimited forgiveness remains unmitigated. Paul holds himself liable for the slave's possible violations. Out of friendship and shared christian dedication, Paul charges Philemon to accept Onesimus as a beloved "brother." But even if this is unacceptable to Philemon, Onesimus is, in fact, in a new and deeper relationship with Philemon: they are related "in the Lord." Onesimus has become much more to both Philemon and Paul "in the Lord" (v.16 cf. 1 Cor 7:20-24; Col 3:11). Paul wishes to derive some "benefit" not only from Onesimus' new status but from Paul's own similar relationship with Philemon "in the Lord" (v.20).

In Christ, "there is neither Jew nor Greek, slave nor free, there is neither male nor female" (Gal 3:28). All are one in the Lord. That is why Philemon can no longer decide on a human basis for he, like Onesimus and Paul himself, has been transformed into a new creation (2 Cor 5:17) and their relationships are likewise on a new level. Any ownership involved, any debts acquired, any wrongs committed, all are changed with the conversion of the heart. Just as Phile-mon is himself Paul's brother, so Onesimus has become kin in the spirit. Just as Philemon has brought joy to Paul's heart by bringing refreshment to the hearts of the saints (v.7), so Paul again challenges him to refresh his own heart in Christ (v.20).

I AM HOPING THROUGH YOUR PRAYERS TO BE GRANTED TO YOU.
(21-25).

> [21]Confident of your obedience, I write to you, knowing that you will do even more than I say. [22]At the same time prepare a guest room for me, for I am hoping through your prayers to be granted to you.
>
> [23]Epaphras, my fellow prisoner in Christ Jesus, sends greetings to you, [24]and so do Mark, Aristarchus, Demas, and Luke, my fellow workers.
>
> [25]The grace of the Lord Jesus Christ be with your spirit.

Paul is not reverting to his appeal to his own authority (cf. v.8) but to the "obedience," the listening of Philemon's Christian heart. Obedience is primarily a Pauline word in the New Testament (cf. Rom 1:5; 5:19; 6:16; 15:18; 16:19, 20; 2 Cor 7:15; 10:5,6: Philemon 21). Philemon will have many problems executing the gospel's demands at Paul's ardent prompting. Paul writes considerately as one who cares enormously that Philemon as well as Onesimus will suffer because of the conviction his own sensitive heart renders.

Paul has expressed apprehension at letting Onesimus depart: he would prefer to have his companionship, his support, and the comfort of his help in his imprisonment. Onesimus risks his life as a fugitive slave in an alien culture and faces a very uncertain future at the mercy of a master he seems to have wronged. Philemon risks financial and social ostracism if he frees Onesimus and spiritual bankruptcy if he does not. Paul expresses confidence in his brother Christian while also sending him the supporting and challenging news of an upcoming visit. Obviously while he expresses confidence, he also reveals his sensitivity to the nearly impossible position in which he places Philemon. He seems to realize that a resolution of this predicament may require a certain amount of time and support. Philemon's prayers are subtly requested so that Paul may soon be able to come to reinforce his demands. With the sensitivity of a pastor, Paul seems to know that Philemon will comply with his appeal but he also realizes at what cost.

Touchingly, Paul asks for hospitality. The apostle's writings as well as the gospels show how close the virtue of hospitality is to the heart of the Christian message (Rom 12:13; 1 Cor 11:17-34; cf. the importance of the banquets in the gospels, Mk 2:18; Lk 7:36-50; 9:13-17; 19:1-10; Mt 22:1-14). Those who respond to the needs of the saints seem to especially appreciate the core of Jesus' teaching. While it may be heroic or admirable to rise to the demands of the faraway crowds, the insistent gospel mandate is to "Love your neighbor," or in John's words, "Love one another." At times the demands of our own communities press us to greater generosity than strangers do. The call for greater charity comes from those we live with and those to whom we are accountable and who might be dependent on us.

Paul's companions are the same as those "saved" in Col 4:9-14, except that Col 4:11 adds "Jesus who is called Justus." Paul continues giving directives to others in vv.15-17. This is one of the reasons Philemon has so often been connected with Colossians. Since we know little about Epaphras, it is impossible to decide whether this is the same person as the bearer of gifts to Paul from the Philippians and the probable carrier of Paul's letter of encouragement and thanks back to Philippi. Mark could be the John Mark, son of Mary (Acts 12:12,25; 15:37) and the cousin of Barnabas (Col 4:10; Acts 15:39). Aristarchus is mentioned in Col 4:10-11 and Acts 27:2; 9:29 and 30:4 as a companion to Paul setting out on Paul's voyage to Rome. Demas is mentioned as loving the present world in 2 Tim 4:10; he returned to Thessalonica, probably his home. Luke is traditionally identified as the evangelist, author of Acts and possible companion of Paul on his journey to Macedonia (Acts 16:10), Jerusalem (Acts 21:15) and Rome (cf. Acts 27:2).

Paul's letter ends with the expected benediction, "The grace of the Lord Jesus Christ be with your Spirit."

ANNOTATED READING LIST

1. ON PHILIPPIANS

Joseph A. Fitzmyer, S.J., "The Letter to the Philippians," *Jerome Biblical Commentary*, pp. 247-253.

Admirably packed with Old Testament allusions that provide the background for Paul's thought. Especially useful for getting one's bearings on the evolution of Paul's theology in Philippians.

J. Gnilka, *The Epistle to the Philippians* (London: Sheed & Ward, 1970).

Readable and comprehensive, this commentary combines good scholarship with a genuine pastoral concern to make Paul understandable to as wide an audience as possible.

R.P. Martin, *Carmen Christi*. Philippians 2:5-11 in Recent Interpretation and in the Setting of Early Christian Worship (Cambridge: University Press, 1967).

Scholarly treatment of various interpretations of Philippians' Christological hymn. Has to be taken into account if the complexities of this passage are to be appreciated.

————, *The Epistle of Paul to the Philippians* (London: The Tyndale Press, 1959).

A stimulating, creative commentary that betrays respect for Paul's love of the church. Paul, apostle and pastor, emerges also as a great-hearted Christian.

Marvin R. Vincent, *Epistle to the Philippians and to Philemon* (Edinburgh: T. & T. Clark, 1955).

First published in 1897, this commentary is eloquent testimony to the thorough, perceptive work done by our exegetical ancestors. A classic, this continues to be helpful and provocative.

2. ON PHILEMON

James T. Burtchaell, *Philemon's Problem*. The Daily Dilemma of the Christian (Chicago: ACTA Foundation, 1973)
>   Demonstrates the relevance of Philemon for the present day. Provocative and forceful.

Joseph A. Fitzmyer, S.J., "The Letter to Philemon," *Jerome Biblical Commentary*. Raymond E. Brown, S.S., Joesph A. Fitzmyer, S.J., Roland E. Murphy O. Carm., (eds.) (Englewood Cliffs: Prentice-Hall, Inc., 1968), pp. 332-333.
>   Short, direct. Highlights the significance of this epistle for the contemporary world.

A. Stoger, *The Epistle to Philemon* (London: Sheed & Ward, 1970).
>   Philemon is relevant for all times. Although it portrays a situation somewhat remote from our own, it demonstrates the force and authenticity of the gospel message. This commentary strengthens the link between Paul's message and our own times.

3. GENERAL WORKS ON PAUL

The following lists works that provide background on the life and works of the apostle:

F.F. Bruce, *Paul, Apostle of the Heart Set Free* (Grand Rapids: Eerdmans, 1977).
>   Not only a pastoral portrayal of Paul but a good introduction to each of his writings. Readily accessible, readable and comprehensive. One of the best, more recent studies on Paul.

Nils A. Dahl, *Studies in Paul*. Theology for the Early Christian Mission (Minneapolis: Augsburg Publishing House, 1977).
>   Collection of articles previously published, primarily in Scandinavian journals, now made more readily accessible. Excellent survey of the broad outlines of Paul's thought.

Joseph A. Fitzmyer, S.J., "The Gospel in the Theology of Paul,"
Interpretation (xxxiii, 4), 1979, pp. 339-350.
   Examines Paul's use of *evangelion*, the main characteristics
   of "gospel" in Paul, the origin and background of this term.
   Clear, concise.
John L. McKenzie, *Light on the Epistles* (Chicago: The Thomas
More Association, 1975).
   Abbreviated commentaries on all of the New Testament
   epistles. Useful for gaining a perspective on the relationship
   between them. Very general.
Wayne A. Meeks (ed.), *The Writings of St. Paul* (New York:
W.W. Norton & Company, Inc. 1972).
   Includes introductions and annotated texts of the Pauline
   literature as well as critical essays by classic and contemporary interpreters. Important for getting a cross section of
   the various ways Paul has been interpreted in history and
   for highlighting some of the main currents of debate regarding major themes in Paul.